THE CONVERGENCE OF TRADITIONS

CONTEMPORARY THEOLOGY

EDITOR: Elmer O'Brien, S.J.

VOLUME II

THE CONVERGENCE
OF TRADITIONS

Orthodox, Catholic, Protestant

Edited by
Elmer O'Brien, S.J.

HERDER AND HERDER

1967
HERDER AND HERDER NEW YORK
232 Madison Avenue, New York 10016

Nihil obstat: Thomas J. Beary, Censor Librorum
Imprimatur: Robert F. Joyce, Bishop of Burlington
July 17, 1967

Contents

Editor's Note

The following pages reproduce the position papers read at the Second Annual Contemporary Theology Institute, Loyola College, Montreal. Designed to present the theological heritages of Orthodoxy, Catholicism, and Protestantism in accord with the Institute's theme of the year, "The Convergence of Traditions," they initiated and sustained theological discussion of a quality which one would wish to see more generally widespread. Hence their publication now.

One of the participants, Professor Oberman, found it personally more congenial to write papers of greater length and of more detailed documentation than the format of the Institute required and then to edit them down during the actual delivery. This is mentioned here lest the reader conclude from the resultant diversity of the participants' papers that Professor Oberman is long-winded or Professors Schmemann and Daniélou are short on scholarship. The explanation, rather, is one which does honor to all three.

THE CONVERGENCE OF TRADITIONS

The Orthodox Tradition

ALEXANDER SCHMEMANN

THE CHURCH

One of the greatest "ecumenical" difficulties of the Orthodox
Church is that her thought forms and "terms of reference" are
different from those of the West. And, since the ecumenical
movement was shaped primarily by Western theological presuppositions and antecedents, its Orthodox particpants were, from the
very beginning, forced to express their positions and "points of
view" within a theological framework alien to, or at least different
from, the Orthodox tradition. This is especially true of ecclesiology. The Orthodox East has not been challenged either by the
politico-ecclesiological controversies typical of the Western Middle Ages or by the Reformation. It remained free, therefore, from
the "polemical" and "definitional" ecclesiology which underlies
the Western *De Ecclesia*, whether in its Roman Catholic or
Protestant form, and which conditions to a great degree the ecumenical debate on the Church. In our own "sources"—the Fathers, the Councils, the Liturgy—we do not find any formal definition of the Church and this is not because of any lack of ecclesiological interest and consciousness, but because the Church—in the
Orthodox approach to her—does not exist (and therefore cannot
be defined) apart from the very content of her life. The Church,
in other terms, is not an "essence" or "being" distinct, as such,
from God, man, and the world, but is the very reality of *Christ in
us* and *us in Christ,* a new mode of God's presence and action in

11

his creation, of creation's life in God. She is God's gift and man's response and appropriation of this gift, union and unity, knowledge, communion and transfiguration. And, since apart from the "content" the "form" has no meaning (cf. the reluctance of Orthodox theologians to discuss problems of "validity"), Orthodox ecclesiology rather than looking for precise definitions or forms, conditions and modalities, is an attempt to present an *icon* of the Church as *life in Christ*—an icon, which to be adequate and true, must draw on all the aspects and not only on the institutional aspects of the Church. For the Church is an *institution*, but she is also a *mystery*; and it is mystery that gives meaning and life to institution and is, therefore, the object of ecclesiology.

Such an attempt must probably begin with the Church as *new* creation. Orthodox ecclesiology traditionally sees the beginning of the Church in Paradise and her life as the manifestation of the Kingdom of God. "The history of the Church begins with the history of the world. The very creation of the world can be seen as preparation for the creation of the Church because the end for which the kingdom of nature was established is in the Kingdom of Grace" (Metropolitan Philaret of Moscow). Thus, the basic dimensions of Orthdox ecclesiology are cosmical and eschatological.

On the one hand, in Christ, the Incarnate Son of God, the new Adam, creation finds not only redemption and reconciliation with God but also its fulfillment. Christ is the Logos, the Life of all life, and this life, which was lost because of sin, is restored and communicated in Christ, in his Incarnation, death, Resurrection, and glorification, to man and through him to the whole creation. Pentecost, the descent of the Holy Spirit who is Giver of Life, is not a mere establishment of an institution endowed with specific powers and authorities. It is the inauguration of the new age, the beginning of life eternal, the revelation of the Kingdom which is "joy and peace in the Holy Spirit." The Church is the continuing presence of Pentecost as power of sanctification and transfiguration of all life, as *grace* which is knowledge of God, communion with him, and, in him with all that exists. The Church is creation as renewed by Christ and sanctified by the Holy Spirit.

12

But, on the other hand, the Kingdom which Christ inaugurates and the Holy Spirit fulfills, is *not of this world*. "This world," by rejecting and condemning Christ, has condemned itself and no one, therefore, can enter the Kingdom without, in a real sense, dying to the world, i.e., rejecting it in its self-sufficiency, without putting all faith, hope, and love in the "age to come," in the "day without evening" which will dawn at the end of time. "You are dead and your life is hid with Christ in God" (Col. 3:3). This means that although the Church abides in the world, her real life is a constant expectation and anticipation of the world to come, a preparation for it, a passage into reality which in this world can be experienced only as future, as promise and token of things yet to come. The fruits of the Spirit—joy, peace, holiness, vision, knowledge—are *real*, but their reality is that of the joy which a traveler has when at the end of a long journey he finally sees the beautiful city where he is going—into which, however, he must yet enter. The Church reveals and truly bestows now the Kingdom which is *to come*, and creation becomes new when it dies to itself as "this world" and becomes thirst and hunger for the consummation of all things in God.

It is the mystery of the Church as new creation in its two dimensions—the cosmical and eschatological—that reveals to us the meaning and structure of the Church as *institution*. The nature of the institution can be termed *sacramental*, and this means not only a given or static interdependence between the visible and the invisible, nature and grace, the material and the spiritual, but also, and primarily, the dynamic essence of the Church as *passage* from the old into the new, from this world into the world to come from the kingdom of nature, into the Kingdom of Grace. The Church, as visible society and organization, belongs to this world; she is truly a part of it. And she must belong to it because she is "instituted" to represent and to stand for the world, to assume the whole creation. It belongs thus to the very "institution" of the Church to be a people, a community, a family, an organization, a nation, a hierarchy, to assume, in other words, all the natural forms of human existence in the world, in time and space. She is in organic continuity with the whole of human life,

13

with the totality of human history. She is the *pars pro toto* of the whole creation. Yet, she is all this in order to reveal and manifest the true meaning of creation as fulfillment in Christ, to announce to the world its end and the inauguration of the Kingdom. The "institution" is thus the sacrament of the Kingdom, the means by which the Church always *becomes what she is*, always fulfills herself as the One, Holy, Catholic, and Apostolic Church, as the Body of Christ and the Temple of the Holy Spirit, as the new life of the new creation. The basic act of this fulfillment, and therefore the true "form" of the Church, is the Eucharist—the sacrament in which the Church performs the passage, the *passover*, from this world into the Kingdom, and offers in Christ the whole creation to God and sees it as "heaven and earth full of his Glory" and partakes of Christ's immortal life at his table in his Kingdom.

This sacramental nature of the Church reveals the real meaning of the universally accepted *notae* by which we confess the Church to be One, Holy, Catholic, and Apostolic. Each of them applies to both the institution and its fulfillment, the form and the content, the promise and its realization. The Church is one, holy, catholic, and apostolic, and she must constantly fulfill herself as oneness, holiness, catholicity, and apostolicity. Her visible oneness is to be realized as the very content of the new life—"that they may be one as we are one"—as the unity of all in God and with God. The objective holiness of her life—the gifts of grace and sanctification which pour from all her acts—is to be fulfilled and realized in personal holiness of her members. The catholicity—the absolute fullness of the Gospel she announces and the life she communicates—is to grow into the "wholeness" of the faith and life of each community, of each Christian and of the whole Church. Her apostolicity—her identity in time and space with the *pleroma* of the Church manifested at Pentecost—is to be preserved whole and undistorted by every generation, always and everywhere.

In this world, the One, Holy, Catholic, and Apostolic Church manifests itself as a plurality of churches, each one of which is a *part* and a *whole*. It is a part because only in unity with all churches and in obedience to the universal Truth can it be the

14

Church; yet it is also a whole because in each church by virtue of her unity with the One, Holy, Catholic, and Apostolic Church, the whole Christ is present, the fullness of grace is given, the catholicity of new life is revealed.

The visible unity of all churches as the One, Holy, Catholic, and Apostolic Church is expressed and preserved in the unity of faith, the unity of sacramental structure, and the unity of life. The unity of faith has its norm and content in the universal tradition. The unity of sacramental structure is preserved through the Apostolic Succession which is the visible and objective continuity of the Church's life and order in time and space. The unity of life manifests itself in the active concern of all churches for each other and of all of them together for the Church's mission in the world.

The organ of unity in the Church is the episcopate. "The Church is in the Bishop." This means that in each church the personal ministry of the bishop is to preserve the fullness of the Church, i.e., her identity and continuity with the One, Holy, Catholic, and Apostolic Church; to be the teacher of the universal traditions; the offerer of the Eucharist which is the Sacrament of unity; and the pastor of the people of God on its pilgrimage to the Kingdom. By virtue of his consecration by other bishops and of his belonging to the universal episcopate, he *re-presents*, makes present and unites his church to all churches and *re-presents* all other churches, and therefore the whole Church, to his own church. In him, each church is thus truly a part of the whole Church and the whole Church is truly present in each church. In the Orthodox tradition, the unity of the episcopate, and especially the organ of this unity, a synod, or council of bishops, is the supreme expression of the Church's teaching and pastoral function—the inspired mouth of the whole Church. But, "the Bishop is in the Church" and this means that neither one bishop nor the episcopate as a whole is above the Church, or (to quote here a famous formula) acts and teaches *ex sese et non ex consensu Ecclesiae*. It is rather his complete identification with and his total obedience to the *consensus Ecclesiae*, to her teaching, life, and holiness, as well as

15

his organic unity with the people of God, that makes the bishop the teacher and the guardian of the truth. For in the Church no one is without the Holy Spirit, and according to the Encyclical of Eastern Patriarchs, the preservation of the truth is entrusted to the whole people of the Church. Thus, the Church is *hierarchical* and *conciliary* and the two principles are not only not opposed to each other but are in their interdependence essential for the full expression of the mystery of the Church.

The One, Holy, Catholic, and Apostolic Church must necessarily exist in the world as an orderly and visibly united Church Universal, and it is the function and charism of the *primacies* to serve as centers of communion, unity, and coordination. There exist local and regional primacies (metropolitans, patriarchs) and a universal primacy. Orthodox ecclesiology has never denied that traditionally the latter belonged to the Church of Rome. It is, however, the interpretation of this primacy in terms of a personal infallibility of the Roman Pontiff and of his universal jurisdictional power that led to its rejection by the Orthodox East.

The Orthodox Church claims to have preserved unaltered and full the Faith and the traditions "once delivered unto the Saints." In face of the tragic divisions among Christians, she affirms that the only way to reunion is the restoration of that *unity of faith* which alone enables each church to see all other churches as the same and One, Holy, Catholic, and Apostolic Church.

The Church is both *in statu patriae* and *in statu viae.* As "Christ in us," as the manifestation of the Kingdom and the sacrament of the age to come, her life is already filled with the "joy and peace of the Holy Spirit" and it is this paschal joy that she expresses and receives in worship, in the holiness of her members, and in the communion of saints. As "we in Christ," she is in pilgrimage and expectation, in repentance and struggle. And above everything else, she is *mission*, for the belonging to the world to come and the joy which, in Christ, has entered the world and the vision of the transfigured world are given to her so that she may be in this world witness to Christ and may save and redeem in him the whole creation.

16

SCRIPTURE

Isolated for centuries from the Christian West and its controversies, the Orthodox Church has never really "lived through" or made her own the *Biblical Problem* as it developed in the West—first, as the question of the Bible's authority (*sola Scriptura*, etc.); second, as the question of biblical criticism. The absence of any serious challenge to the place traditionally occupied by Holy Scripture in the Church has prevented the Orthodox East from any "explicitation" of that place, from any elaborate definition of Scripture in its nature and in its relation to the Church. To a Westerner, therefore, the traditional Orthodox attitude toward Scripture may appear as a pre-critical "naïve realism." But the Orthodox Church, if she does not think too much *about* Scripture, knows it to be the very heart of her life, the very source of her faith and knowledge of God. It is with this living experience of Scripture that one must begin the description of the Orthodox approach to it.

In the Orthodox Church, Scripture is not primarily the authority to be quoted in support of this or that dogmatical or moral proposition, nor a supreme *locus theologicus* for matters doctrinal or ethical. Scripture is, first of all, a *nourishment*, a real communion with God, a way of life in him. Our theology does not start with abstract notions of inspiration, inerrancy, authority, etc. In the living experience of the Church, it is not the inclusion of a book in the canon that makes it "Holy Scripture"; rather it is included in the canon because the Church has heard the Word of God in it. The Church and Scripture are not two distinct "authorities" justifying and confirming each other. They are one and the same source of life, knowledge, and communion, the same Word of God spoken to us and making his abode in us. And it is by being nourished by the Word of God in Scripture that the Church *knows* and appropriates the inexhaustible "meanings" of Scripture. It is by using it that she finds life in it.

Orthodox theology is reluctant about any "reduction" of the Scriptures to one theme, such as "History of Salvation," for exam-

17

ple, or to one method and theory of scriptural interpretation. What makes Holy Scripture a unique source of revelation and, indeed, *the* Bible, *the* Book, is precisely its inexhaustible richness, its all-embracing character. The Bible is a whole world in which the Christian really lives and which he never finishes discovering. As Revelation, it reveals not only some doctrinal propositions about God and his acts in history; it reveals, so to speak, the whole of creation, the whole of life, the whole of being in all its depth. "He who has departed from the fantasies of heresy," writes Clement of Alexandria, "and, hearing the Scriptures, has dedicated his life to the Truth, such a man becomes a god. For we hold as the principle of our knowledge the Lord who, through the Prophets, the Gospels, and the Holy Apostles, leads us in a thousand ways *from the beginning to the end of Science.* If anybody supposed he needed anything else as principle, then there would be no principle left indeed. He then who spontaneously believes in the Lord's Scripture and Voice, ought to be believed" (*Stromateis*, Bk. VII, chap. 13). From this point of view, there is no special "biblical theology"; all theology is biblical, not only in the sense that it has in Scripture its proof and criterion (as the Orthodox Church firmly maintains), but the whole life of the Church, her whole teaching is a perpetual commentary of the Bible, of the Truth revealed in it. Likewise, the Orthodox Church has never defined and sanctioned any one particular method of interpreting the Scripture, for there is no end to this interpretation, and no single approach or method can exhaust it.

One principle, however, is clear: the real framework of this interpretation, the *life* of Scripture, is the Church. Tradition in Orthodox theology is not distinguished from or opposed to Scripture because, on the one hand, Scripture itself is a part of Tradition, of what we receive in the Church, and, on the other hand, the whole Tradition is nothing else but the *reading* and the *appropriation* of Scripture in the life of the Church. Tradition, thus, is neither a complement, an addition to Scripture ("the oral teaching of Christ not recorded in writing by his immediate disciples," as it is sometimes defined), nor a simple "systematization" of biblical "data" and "materials." It is a living interpretation of

18

divine Revelation not only in words and propositions but in the whole life of the Church. It is the reading of Scripture through the "mind of Christ" and in the light of the Holy Spirit bestowed upon the Church. In this sense, the "proof from the Bible" is not a mere quotation, a text found as justification, but the inner consistency of all truth, life and action of the Church with the scriptural Revelation. "Homoousios" was condemned by the enemies of St. Athanasius of Alexandria as a nonscriptural term; yet it was finally accepted by the Church as the best means of expressing precisely the scriptural Revelation about God and the Incarnation. And, reversely, the real meaning of Scripture cannot be grasped outside the living continuity of the Church—(and this means) outside Tradition. It is only from within the Church, from within her communion with Christ and the Holy Spirit, that the words of Scripture can be heard and received as the Word of God.

From within the Church means, first of all, in the liturgy, in the visible *ecclesia,* in the act by which and in which a Christian community constitutes itself as the Church. The liturgy is the real source and criterion of all scriptural interpretation and therefore of all theology because liturgy is the entrance of the Church into the dimensions of Christ, its fulfillment as the Body of Christ. Historically, theology began as the preaching of the Word within the Christian assembly, for it is here that the same Holy Spirit acts in the one who preaches and in those who receive his preaching. The interpretation of Scripture—the essential teaching function of the Church—is rooted thus in the reality of the Church and this means in the act which manifests the unity of the Head and the Body, which fulfills the communion in the Holy Spirit.

Preaching, however, is not the only link between the liturgy and Scripture. Rather, one can say that the whole liturgy is the preaching and the unfolding of Scripture, and, even more, that the liturgy is the very fulfillment of Scripture in the Church. The very structure of Christian worship, its language, its rhythm, its whole ethos are biblical in the deepest sense of this word so that neither can the liturgy be understood and truly experienced without Scripture nor can Scripture be fully appropriated without the liturgy. Thus, for example, the meaning of water and oil in Baptism; of

19

the bread and wine in the Eucharist; of the essential liturgical use of time, light, darkness; the basic rites of gathering, entrance, blessing; the key liturgical terms such as "glory," "amen," "alleluia," etc.; and finally the entire language of the liturgy simply cannot be grasped or heard in its true significance by someone whose mind and soul are not "imbued with Scripture to the point of reading everything in the world through it and finding the whole world in it" (L. Bouyer).

An Orthodox does not understand very well the much-discussed problem of biblical "relevance" and "hermeneutics" because it is the liturgy which makes the Bible relevant to him just as the relevance of the Bible presupposes his submersion into the liturgical life of the Church. The Book of Exodus, for example, is not only an "appropriate" reading for Holy Week; it really shows and reveals its dogmatical meaning. And, when on the Great and Holy Saturday at the beginning of the Paschal Vigil the Church triumphantly intones the canticle of Moses—". . . for he has glorified himself"—this canticle, sung within the context and the dialectics of Holy Week, explains how and why the grave of Holy Friday is being transformed into the life-giving tomb and what the death of Christ means better and more fully than the innumerable scholastic theologies of the Atonement and Redemption. It is thus in and through the liturgy that Scripture becomes the *nourishment* of the Church, its real communion with the Word of God, and it is, of course, in the light of this liturgical experience, and in reference to it, that the Christian reads Scripture and meditates upon its meaning and makes it his daily spiritual food.

One example crucial for the understanding of Orthodoxy illustrates better than any abstract formula the use of Scripture and its fruit in the life of the Church. It is the veneration of Mary—the Mother of God, the *Theotokos*. To many Protestants who claim that they abide by the principle of *"sola Scriptura,"* Mariology appears as the classical example of a deviation from Scripture as a nonscriptural tradition. From within the Orthodox tradition, however, the veneration of Mary is a self-evident fruit of the "search of Scripture." It is sufficient to read the texts of the great Mariological feasts (Nativity, Presentation in the Temple, Purification, Dormition) to see how biblical they are, how deeply rooted in the biblical Revelation about God, man, and the world. The Gospel tells us that Jesus had a mother, but it is the whole of Scripture that supplies us with the meaning of that Woman, Virgin, Mother, Bride, just as it reveals why water, bread, wine, and oil are to become the means of man's entrance into the Kingdom of God. The Feast of the Nativity of the Theotokos, for example, is formally a nonscriptural feast, for this event is not even mentioned in the Scriptures. But in the light of all that Scripture reveals to us about generations and families of the Old Testament, in the light also of this birth being the end of the whole history of salvation, it is indeed quite scriptural to contemplate the birth of the one who had to give our humanity to the Son of God and to rejoice in the meaning of that event. The poetical details of Mary's entrance into the Temple are, to be sure, taken from the Apocrypha, but this does not alter the meaning of the relationship between her as the living Temple and the hand-made Temple of Jerusalem, and to contemplate this relationship as the beginning of the great mystery of the Incarnation.

"Search the Scriptures . . . they are they that testify to me" (Jn. 5:39). Orthodox theology understands this text not only in its narrow, technically "Christocentric" sense—as a prophecy of the coming of Christ and a record of the history of salvation leading to Christ. It understands it also in relationship to Christ as the Logos, the Word of God in whom is the Life, and, therefore, the meaning and the end of all that exists. It is this Word of God, this light and life, that fills Scripture and makes it the unique Revelation of God and a testimony to Christ. The whole of Scripture testifies to Christ because he is the alpha and omega of all being. In other terms, Scripture is "Christocentric," not because it speaks allegorically or typologically *about* Christ, but because it reveals, manifests, and announces that life in God, that meaning of all creation in God, that joy about God and obedience to him, and finally that glory of God which point to Christ as to their fulfillment and which he, the Incarnate God, bestows upon us as his Kingdom. Scripture, thus, is truly an *icon* of Christ.

All this does not mean that the Orthodox Church rejects the

21

scientific or critical study of Scripture, but this study can be fruitful only if Scripture is not artificially separated from the Church and from her living tradition. For the ultimate key to the meaning of Scripture is in the mind of the Church illuminated and guided into all truth by the Holy Spirit.

TRADITION AND TRADITIONS

The Russian theologian Vladimir Lossky defined Tradition as "the life of the Holy Spirit in the Church." The constant and unanimous affirmation by Orthodox theology that Tradition is the source of faith, the principle of unity, and the norm of all life in the Church, must be seen and understood in the light of that definition. First of all, Tradition is not to be simply identified with *authority*, with a blind and mechanical obedience to the past, considered as absolute norm. Rather, it can be compared to the memory of a man for its real function is to transform and integrate the past into the present and thus to assure the very continuity of life, the identity of the living consciousness. Traditionalism, as blind conservatism and attachment to forms rather than to content and meaning, is alien to the Church and may even lead into schism (one recalls the opposition of the conservatives to the "homoousios" in the fourth century, or the schism of the Russian Old Believers in the seventeenth century). In the second place, Tradition is not "fixed" in the sense of a precise catalogue of definitions, doctrines, forms, and norms; and the very existence of "symbolical books" is seriously questioned by Orthodox theologians. The Orthodox Church is reluctant to formulate Tradition as a "minimum" which then could be defined as "necessary and sufficient." This would be in absolute contradiction of the understanding of Tradition as the life of the Holy Spirit in the Church—the Spirit who lives and acts in the Church always, today as yesterday, and inspires all her life and makes it a continuity of life, faith, and love and not a mechanical repetition of the past.

Tradition does not exclude either new formulations or new forms of the Church's life. It means only that such new formula-

22

tions will be the formulations of the same eternal and unchanging truth inspired by the same eternal and unchanging Spirit and therefore will never be in contradiction of that which has been accepted and received as truth in the Church. And it means that the new forms will be forms of the same living Church and therefore the expressions of the same life.

Although Tradition is one and indivisible and can be truly understood only in its totality and wholeness, one can distinguish various strata or elements within it. Not all elements are of equal value; not all perform the same function. The first, most important, and, in a certain sense, all-embracing and normative element of Tradition is *Holy Scripture.* Orthodox theology does not oppose Tradition to Scripture, does not "number" them as separate sources of faith. But it certainly "numbers" Scripture as the first and essential expression of Tradition. Scripture is the inner source and norm of Tradition, being its very foundation. On the one hand, it is Tradition which *receives* Scripture in the Church (e.g., the establishing of the canon of the New Testament) but, on the other hand, it is Scripture that controls Tradition in its internal consistency and catholicity. In a sense the whole Tradition is an inspired reading of Scripture by the Church, the revelation and interpretation of its meaning by the Holy Spirit abiding in the Church. Holy Scripture, thus, truly posits the necessity of Tradition, for if Scripture contains the living and ever-acting Word of God, it must of necessity be constantly received and appropriated by the Church, and this reception and appropriation, this inspired reading of Scripture *is* Tradition.

Then comes dogmatic tradition—the dogmas as defined by the councils of the Church and the general ecclesiological consensus. Orthodox theology attaches a special importance to the councils in which it sees the very organ of the Church's teaching ministry— indeed the organ of the Holy Spirit. The definition of a dogma, however, does not mean that the latter has been transferred into the category of absolute authorities simply to be repeated and kept as definitions. Dogma is not a mere intellectual proposition requiring nothing but a formal assent and obedience. It is a living and saving truth which must truly shape the life and the mind of the

23

Church and assure the difficult and creative process of "entering into the Truth."

Dogmatic tradition includes the teachings of the Fathers. But, again, the Church has never "canonized" patristic theology in its every word and has not even established a compulsory list of the Fathers and their writings. It is rather the spirit of their theology that the Church considers as belonging to Tradition, the catholicity, i.e., the holiness of their minds, its total identification with the mind of the Church. There exists a world of patristic thought, experience, and vision—a world which the Church *knows* to reveal the right approach to God, man and the world and to be, therefore, a source and a criterion of all true catholic theology in the Church. The *consensus patrum* is not an artificially isolated minimum of the Fathers' statements in which they all agree, but rather the oneness of the reality to which they all belong and within which they think, move, and live.

Liturgical tradition has a special significance as both a source of faith and a way to understand the function of Tradition in the Church. The liturgy, and more specifically the Sacraments, is the very means of the Church's fulfillment as the Body of Christ, as continuing Pentecost. It is therefore in and through the liturgy that the past really becomes present, is actualized and communicated as a "now." It is the liturgy and the Sacraments that reveal and confirm the truth and efficiency of those events (Incarnation, Resurrection, Glorification) which otherwise would remain doctrinal "propositions." It is thus in the liturgy that Tradition "comes alive" and is received as a living reality, as event and not only as doctrine. One can therefore understand the liturgy as the organ of the Church's knowledge of Tradition.

But liturgy is not only the knowledge of Tradition; it is also an essential element of Tradition itself. There are doctrines and teachings which belong to Tradition and which are formulated and manifested almost exclusively by means of the liturgy. The two obvious examples here would be Mariology and ecclesiology. The entire "knowledge" of Mary, the *Theotokos*, comes, so to speak, from liturgical communion with her. Orthodox Mariology is even somewhat reluctant to systematize the Mariological "data"

24

supplied by the liturgy, as if the only proper way to understand her were precisely in liturgical contemplation and communion. Likewise, the proper elaboration and "explicitation" of ecclesiology is, from the Orthodox point of view, impossible without looking at it through the liturgy, and more especially through the Eucharist, which is the Sacrament of the Church, the act in which the Church fulfills and manifests itself as the Body of Christ, "mysterion" of the Kingdom of God. For example, the very fact that the Sacrament of Order is inseparable from the Eucharist tells more about it than volumes of investigations in the "nature of mystery." And, finally, the liturgical texts themselves which constitute the prayer of the Church have always been understood as self-evident manifestations of Tradition.

The liturgy includes as its necessary element the tradition of Christian art, and especially iconography. Iconography has always been in the Orthodox Church an important expression of Tradition for in the Orthodox teaching, as it has been formulated by the Fathers who fought the great iconoclastic controversy of the eighth and ninth centuries, the *icon* is not a mere "visual aid" or a pious decoration of a temple. It is truly an "epiphany"—a manifestation of the Holy Spirit. It is, in the words of a Russian philosopher, a "vision of God in colors." It is for the Church, therefore, as much a source of knowledge and faith as its fruit. The famous icon of the Holy Trinity by the Russian mediaeval icon painter, Andrew Rublev, is not only an "illustration" of Orthodox Triadology, but a direct *vision* of the Trinity and a communication of that vision. *Mutatis mutandis*, the same can be said of the tradition of *liturgical music*. Liturgy is primarily "singing unto the Lord" and the new song of the New Creation is an essential way of participating in the life of the Church. Therefore, for an Orthodox, the temple and all that it includes—worship, icons, music—are truly an *icon* of the Kingdom of God as revealed by Christ, a constant participation in the new age, and therefore the very life in Tradition and Tradition as life.

The Orthodox Church sees in the *canons* an integral part of Tradition. The canons are rules and regulations composed at different times and on different occasions by Church councils and

Fathers and they deal primarily with the order and discipline of Church life. But it would be improper to see them exclusively in terms of discipline, or rather it would be wrong to see in the whole area of ecclesiastical discipline a merely "juridical" codex of external prescriptions. The Orthodox Church has never isolated the canonical tradition as a self-sufficient category of ecclesiastical law, for the canons (not less than the dogmas, although in a different way) reveal and communicate the truth of the Church, her belonging to the Kingdom of Grace; and their first function (which precisely makes them a permanent and unchanging part of Tradition) is to show how the Kingdom of Grace is to be fulfilled and manifested in the empirical life of the Church. One can say that they too are an *icon* of the Church and of our life in the Church, and this applies even to the canons whose literal and direct content does not apply any longer. A canon may deal with a specific situation which does not exist today, but what remains as its permanent value is the truth which is applied to that particular situation and which reveals therefore an essential aspect of the total truth of the Church. It is only through the canonical tradition that we know that a bishop must be consecrated by "all the bishops of a province" or "at least by two or three bishops"; the rule laid down in this canon, if properly understood, contains in it the whole idea of the relationship between churches and their unity as expressed in the unity of the episcopate and is one of the key texts for the understanding of Orthodox ecclesiology. Properly read and interpreted, the canons present a normative description of Christian life and this is what makes them an essential element of Tradition.

The tradition of holiness is equally important. On the one hand, the Saints are the only real witnesses of Christ, of his presence in the Church. They are also our guides and teachers in our own Christian life, in our own effort toward the Kingdom. On the other hand, each one of them and all of them together reveal something of that Kingdom of Grace and of its manifestation in the Church. The tradition of spirituality, its continuity in the Church, is truly the preservation of the Church as an eschatological community whose life cannot be reduced to anything in this world because it is "hid with Christ in God" and is the anticipation and expectation of the Kingdom. The Church is truly a communion of saints because it is communion with the Saints in Christ, and the very concept of Tradition as the life of the Holy Spirit in the Church would be incomplete and one-sided without this "cloud of witnesses" of the Spirit.

To be sure, Tradition is to be distinguished from traditions—from local customs and memories, temporary values, undue absoluteness of secondary values, etc. It is the proper function of theology to be in constant search of the real Tradition and, therefore, be its purification from all that in the empirical life of the Church is constantly obscuring it. Theology thus has a prophetical dimension. It tests all traditions and by exposing the true Tradition makes us again and again free children of God.

SACRAMENTS

One must distinguish *Sacraments* as particular acts or "means of grace" from the *sacramental principle* which underlies them and is rooted in the very nature of the Church. Although Orthodox theology in its post-patristic "Westernizing" form has more or less adopted a scholastic approach toward Sacraments (matter and form, conditions of validity, etc.) the whole framework of the Orthodox liturgical and theological tradition indicates a wider concept of the Sacraments, or to use a patristic term, "mysterion." And it is only on the basis of this wider sacramental theology that one can properly understand the various liturgical acts defined as Sacraments.

The usually accepted theory of Sacraments applies to them the categories of visible and invisible, nature and grace, matter and form. Sacrament is defined as a visible sign of an invisible grace and all Sacraments, therefore, as means of grace. This theory, although not a wrong one, is, to say the least, one-sided, for it neglects and leaves out the fundamental relationship between the Sacraments and the Church and, more precisely, the sacramental nature of the Church herself. The Church is presented as distribu-

27

tor of sacramental grace aimed at personal sanctification and edifi-
cation of her individual members but not as being herself primarily
the *Sacrament of the Kingdom, therefore,* fulfilling herself in and
through Sacraments. What is thus overlooked is the ecclesiological
and eschatological meaning of Sacraments and this, in turn, has a
deep impact on sacramental piety. This piety, instead of being
church-centered, becomes a kind of "private" devotion satisfying
one's individual religious needs. The time has certainly come for a
deep rethinking and even a real "rediscovery" of the traditional
sacramental theology of the Church.

The starting point of such a rediscovery might be a return from
the abstract and rational categories of visible and invisible, nature
and grace, etc., to those which were used in the early Church and
are more adequate to sacramental reality. The early Church
thought of Sacraments not in terms of nature and grace but in
those of the *old* and the *new.* The fundamental "mysterion" of
Christ is that in him begins the *new age* and this new age reveals
the world as the *old age* or "this world." The coming of the Holy
Spirit is not only a high point of grace, it is the inauguration in
this world of the world to come, of the ontologically *new life*—the
life *in Christ;* and the Church, fulfilled on that day of Pentecost, is
thus the presence in this world of the *passage,* the *entrance* into
the new age, of the communion with the world to come. She is, in
other terms, the "mysterion" or the sacrament of the Kingdom.
The Sacrament of Baptism (which has always been an act of
entering into the Church) is primarily an act of passage from the
old into the new; and the most ancient "paradigmata" of the
baptismal initiation—the Crossing of the Red Sea, or Elijah and
Jordan—indicate precisely the dynamic and eschatological understanding of Baptism. Likewise, the great baptismal feast of the
early Church—Pascha—is not so much a historical commemora-
tion of the Resurrection as the *mysterion* of Christ as the Passage—*passover*—from death to life, from this world into the Kingdom, the passover which in Baptism is communicated to us and
whose fruit in the world is the Church. Sacrament can thus be
described as the entrance into and the possession in this world of
things to come, of the Kingdom of God already inaugurated and

fulfilled in Christ's glorification, which, for this world, is still to come. In the early Church the terms *grace* or *sanctification* were inseparable from such an eschatological connotation. They pointed toward the life of the Church as the life of the new *eon* in the Kingdom.

It is of course in the Eucharist, the Sacrament of the Church (and as the Fathers "defined" it, the "Sacrament of Sacraments"), that the sacramental principle finds its full expression and in turn establishes the real dimensions of the sacramental life of the Church. But it is probably in its dealings with the Eucharist that the sacramental theology which developed in the post-patristic age narrowed more than anywhere else the true sacramental perspective.

Having forgotten the ecclesiological and eschatological significance of the Eucharist, having reduced it to one "means of grace" among many, our official theology was bound to limit the theological study of the Eucharist to only two problems: that of the transformation of bread and wine into the Body and Blood of Christ, and that of communion. . . .

. . . But from the standpoint of Tradition, the sacramental character of the Eucharist cannot be artificially narrowed to one act, to one moment of the whole rite. We have an "ordo" in which all parts and all elements are essential, are organically linked together into one sacramental structure. In other words, the Eucharist is a sacrament from the beginning to the end and its fulfillment or consummation is "made possible" by the entire liturgy. Liturgy here is not opposed to sacrament, as "symbol" to "realism" but indeed *is* sacrament: one organic, consistent *passage* in which each step prepares and "makes possible" the following one.

For the Eucharist we have said is a *passage*, a procession, leading the Church into "heaven," into her fulfillment as Kingdom of God. And it is precisely the reality of this passage into the *Eschaton* that conditions the transformation of our offering—bread and wine—into the new food of the new creation, of our meal into the Messianic Banquet. Thus, for example, the coming together of Christians on the Lord's Day, their visible unity "sealed" by the celebrant is already the beginning of the sacrament, the gathering or the transformation of the community *into* the Church. And the *entrance* is not a symbolical representation of Christ going to preach, but a *real* entrance, the beginning of the Church's ascension to the Throne of God, made possible, inaugurated, by the ascension of Christ's humanity. The offertory, the solemn transfer of the gifts of bread and wine to the altar again is not the symbol of Christ's burial or of His entrance into Jerusalem (as the symbolical explanation of worship suggests) but the *real* sacrifice—the transfer of our lives and bodies and of the whole "matter," of the whole creation into Heaven, their integration into the unique and all-embracing sacrifice of all sacrifices, that of Christ. The *prosphora* makes possible the *anaphora*—the lifting up of the Church into her heavenly dimension, her eschatological fulfillment by the *Eucharist*. For Eucharist—"thanksgiving"—is indeed the very content of the redeemed life, the very *reality* of the Kingdom as "peace and joy in the Holy Spirit," the end and the goal of our ascension into heaven. Therefore, the Eucharist *is* consecration and the Fathers called both the prayer of consecration and the consecrated gifts "Eucharist." The insistence of Orthodox theology on the *epiclesis* (the sacramental invocation of the Holy Spirit) is nothing else, in its ultimate significance, than the affirmation that the consecration, i.e., the transformation of bread and wine into the Body and Blood of Christ takes place in the "new eon" of the Holy Spirit. Our earthly food *becomes* the Body and Blood of Christ because it has been assumed, accepted, lifted up, into the "age to come" where Christ is indeed the very life, the very food of all life, and the Church is His Body, "the fullness of Him that filleth all in all" (Eph. 1:23). It is there, finally, that we partake of the food of immortality, are made participants of the Messianic Banquet, of the new Pascha, it is from there "having seen the true light, having received the heavenly spirit" that we return into "this world" ("let us depart in peace") as witnesses of the Kingdom which is "to come." Such is the sacrament of the Church, the "*leitourgia*," which eternally transforms the Church into what she is, makes her the Body of Christ and the temple of the Holy Spirit. (A. Schmemann, "Theology and Eucharist," *St. Vladimir's Seminary Quarterly*, V (1961), 18–20)

The ecclesiological and eschatological nature of the Eucharist (its character as the Sacrament of the Kingdom) elucidates first its relationship with other Sacraments, which in official post-patristic theology are considered as separate "means of grace" virtually independent of one another. This type of theology begins with a general theory of Sacraments and then applies it to every particular Sacrament. As to Tradition, it follows exactly the opposite order. It begins with concrete liturgical acts which not only are organically related to each other but necessarily refer to the Eucharist which alone fulfills and reveals their true meaning as Sacraments. I already mentioned Baptism which in the early Church is explained not in terms of "original sin" and "sanctifying grace" but as the entrance into the Church, and therefore a truly eschatological transfer from the old life, which is death, into the death which is life. But this transfer finds its necessary end in the Eucharist, for Baptism opens the doors of the Church which fulfills herself in the eucharistic banquet. The Sacrament of Penance or repentance ("confession" and "absolution" in terms of official theology) is originally an act of reconciliation with the Church of those who have fallen away from her and therefore again a transfer—a passage—from the death of sin into the Church as reconciliation, as peace—in Christ—with God. It also naturally leads to the Eucharist because *excommunication* is primarily the falling away from the *koinonia*, the communion in Christ. Matrimony is the "transfer" of the natural marriage into the dimension of the Church ("this is a great mystery but I speak of Christ and the Church") and its first *rite* was simply the communion at the Eucharist (the "common cup" has become today a mere symbol of common life). The Sacrament of oil or healing is again the transformation of a defeat (disease) into victory (the victorious sufferings of Christ) and has always been consummated in the paschal joy of the Eucharist (communion of the sick). Finally, the Sacrament of Order by its very celebration within the Eucharist reveals its organic connection with that Sacrament of the Church. All Sacraments, in other words, deal with individual members of the Church but their very purpose is to *integrate* the individual, his life, his particular "leitourgia" or calling, into the Church. The Church is fulfilled in the Eucharist and each Sacrament therefore finds its end, its fulfillment, in the Eucharist.

Being ecclesiological and eschatological, the sacramental principle is, of necessity, also cosmical. This means that it manifests the true nature of the cosmos as it is revealed to us in the Church. The

31

Church is sacrament because in a deep sense the very structure of creation is sacramental. We have defined Sacrament as a passage; yet being a passage, a transfer, it is also a *transformation*. The old life is not replaced by new life; it is transformed into new life. The bread and wine are not replaced by the Body and Blood of Christ; they are *changed* (*metabolein*) into the Body and Blood of Christ. The Church does not replace the world but transforms it into the "new heaven and earth." And the Christian hopes not for the Church but for a New Creation. The Church thus reveals the very nature of creation as *sacramental* matter that is destined from all eternity to *become* the Kingdom of God and a New Creation. To be sure, the Gospel always reminds us that this transformation, this sacramental change, is not by means of a natural evolution, *and* that its unique pattern is that of *death and resurrection*. Every Sacrament is performed by the sign of the Cross. But it is the one who dies who then is risen again and Thomas is called to make sure of that. The new life which shines from the grave is the same life created by God but victorious over death and sin. The world is to die; it has condemned itself to death. But in the Church, in the Sacraments, in the Kingdom of Grace, it is this same world which is made new, risen from death. In the Eucharist the whole world, the whole creation is offered to God: "Thine own of Thine own we offer unto Thee on behalf of all and for all." Not a part but the whole. Christ, the Son of God, assumes the whole of life and offers it to his Father; and when he ascends to heaven it is the whole man and his whole life that are entering with him into the Kingdom of Glory.

The world was thus created in order to *become* the Kingdom of God, to be united with God, to become truly communion with God who fills "all in all." Man was to perform the sacramental change as king and priest of creation, and his whole life was to be one all-embracing eucharist. He lost this life in sin. He separated himself from God. But the eucharistic life was restored to him in Christ and it is this life that the Church gives to us and this is why in the heart of her whole being we find the Eucharist—the Sacrament of the cosmos—the Sacrament of the Kingdom.

GRACE

The difference between the two spiritual worlds—the Christian East and the Christian West—is nowhere more obvious than in the difference between their approaches to grace and, consequently, to the rapport grace-nature. It is very doubtful that "grace" as such, would be the theme of a theological debate among Orthodox theologians, for the East generally considers grace not so much in itself but rather as related to *theosis*—the "deification," which in Orthodox theology constitutes the real goal of Creation, Redemption, and Salvation. The difference of approach toward grace, of the theological elaboration of this doctrine between the Eastern and Western theological traditions, was brought in sharp focus by the famous "Palamite" controversy which opposed, in the fourteenth century on Byzantine soil, the partisans of Western scholasticism (although in its Greek form) to the defenders of "hesychasm," a spiritual and ascetical doctrine common to the whole patristic tradition. The spokesman of this group, St. Gregory Palamas, remains thus the great Orthodox teacher on grace and it is his teaching (although it is really not different except in terminology from the consensus of all Greek Fathers) that formulates the Eastern Orthodox doctrine of grace. In this brief presentation it has to be reduced to *three* main affirmations: (1) the non-created character of grace and its identity with the divine energies; (2) grace as *deification* of man; and (3) the *synergeia* or free cooperation between man and grace necessary for deification.

First of all there is need for an important clarification. "The Orthodox Tradition," writes Professor Lossky, "ignores a 'pure nature' to which grace would be added as a supernatural gift. There does not exist any 'normal' natural state, for grace is implied in the act of creation itself." This means that the sharp opposition between nature and grace on which the whole Western theological tradition is based is alien to the Orthodox East. The real distinction is not between nature and grace but between the non-created

33

and the created. Orthodox theology rejects a "supernatural" order between God and the created world which in terms of Professor Lossky "would be added to the world as another creation." Creation, being creation by God, is in itself an act of grace. Palamas would even admit here the term "created grace" although it could easily be misinterpreted because of the Western usage of the term. It means only that the world not only reflects, in its own created order, the Wisdom and the Glory of God but that it is predestined naturally and, so to speak, normally to be united with God. Created in order to be deified, the world is dynamic, is tending toward its final goal; and there is for the creature no other goal, no other end: it belongs therefore as *telos*, as "predisposition," to nature itself. But then, if there is no created "supernature" but only the world created by God, and God creating the world for deification, grace must, of necessity, be God himself, and such is precisely the fundamental affirmation of Orthodox theology.

But does this not lead to a confusion between God and the world, between the non-created and the created? This question Orthodox theology answers by the classical distinction between the essence of God and his energies. It is important to note, however, that this distinction (which constitutes the heart of Palamite theology) is not an abstract philosophical speculation and also not a strange mystical fantasy as it was characterized for a long time (before a better knowledge of Palamas was made possible by the publication of his works by Fr. John Meyendorff, and the works of V. Lossky, Cyprian Kern, B. Krivoshein, and Meyendorff himself). It is an attempt to find adequate words and categories for an experience of union with God himself which is *the* experience of the Church and which is clearly affirmed in Scripture: *divinae naturae consortes*. The whole experience and teaching of the Church affirms and preserves as its "holy of holies" that man in Christ is truly united to God himself and not to an intermediate "supernature." "God became man to make man God." This soteriological formula of Irenaeus and Athanasius is the basic norm of all theology, of all attempts to express and formulate the Faith and experience of the Church. Yet, another fundamental principle of the Faith is that the nature of God is

34

absolutely inaccessible to man. "One could compile two series of contradictory texts taken from Scripture and the Fathers," writes Lossky, "some affirming the inaccessible character of divine nature and some affirming that God communicates himself, can be really reached and experienced in union." And it is this antinomy, a real and not a theoretical one, which is, in fact, the beginning of theology. As was said above, Orthodox theology preserves this antinomy by a distinction in God between his nature and his energies. In his nature he is absolutely inaccessible but in his energies he enters in communion with creation and truly unites it to himself. The energies or natural operations of God are inseparable from his essence but in them God proceeds *ad extra*, manifests and gives himself to creation. Whatever the value of this terminology, the main point is absolutely clear: it is to maintain the living antinomical character of Christian experience of the *kerygma* which announces that *God is with us*, that in Christ a real union has been achieved—a union which constitutes the very life, the very goal, the very joy of the Church. Whereas the Western tradition seems to bypass the antinomy by insisting on the created character of grace (and thus at least in the eyes of Eastern theology, denies the real union of creature with God), the Orthodox East (in its traditional "apophatic-kataphatic" way of theologizing) keeps together as an evidence of Faith both the absolute inaccessibility of God in his nature, and a real union with him by grace.

The doctrine of grace is inseparable in Orthodox theology from the doctrine of deification, or *theosis*. In the past, this doctrine has been denounced and rejected by many Western theologians (both Roman Catholic and Protestant) as a dangerous slip in the direction of pantheism and confusion of the human with the divine. These fears, however, are not justified. Deification means simply union with God and such is, as said above, the real goal of all that exists but especially of man, the king of creation. The world, created by God, is *ordered* toward such union, but there eternally remains the absolute abyss between the divine nature and the deified human or created nature. The solution of this doctrine is not "mystic" in the sense in which this term is used sometimes in the West. It is in the central Christian doctrine of Incarnation. "The doctrine of deification," writes Professor Meyendorff, "is for Palamas the direct consequence of the historical work of Christ; outside of him divine life remains inaccessible to man." It is made accessible in the Church and especially in the Sacraments. In other words, the doctrine of deification is not different from the doctrine of salvation and sanctification. But, whereas in the West, because of factors which it is impossible to analyze here, the emphasis in soteriology was laid on "salvation *from*. . . ," in the East salvation means not only the restoration of man after his fall, his reconciliation with God, and his justification, but the fulfillment of the fundamental goal of creation that God may be "all in all." And, as such, deification is not the destiny of the "happy few," of a special category of "mystics"; it is, so to speak, the natural end of each Christian and of the whole Church. It is another way to proclaim the central Christian teaching about the Wisdom of God, "new heaven and new earth. . . ."

The third essential aspect of the Orthodox doctrine of grace is the notion of *synergeia,* or free cooperation between God and man in the work of salvation and deification. "The Eastern Tradition has never separated one from another the two realities of grace and of human freedom. They manifest themselves simultaneously and cannot be conceived one without the other" (V. Lossky). St. Gregory of Nyssa writes: "As the grace of God cannot abide in the souls which flee from their salvation, human virtue by itself is not sufficient to elevate to perfection the souls alien to grace . . ." (*De instituto Christiano,* cited in Lossky, *Théologie Mystique,* p. 194). "Grace is thus not a recompense for the merit of human will as Pelagianism would want it to be. Yet, it is not the 'cause' of 'meritorious acts' of our freedom. The crux of the matter lies not in merits but in cooperation, of synergy of two wills, the divine and the human, an accord in which grace . . . finds itself appropriated, is 'acquired' by the human person. The grace is the presence of God in us which requires on our part a constant effort. This effort, however, does not in any way determine grace, just as grace does not move our will as a force which would be alien to it" (Lossky, *ibid.*).

36

It is in the ascetical or spiritual tradition, or rather in the continuity of holiness in the Church, that the Orthodox East finds the self-evident context for its doctrine of grace. The cult of the Saints and especially its living center, the veneration of the *Theotokos*, the Mother of God, is above all "Theocentric" and "Christocentric." The Saint is a *martus*, a witness of the presence of God in the Church, the one in whom divine life has manifested itself, yet not in spite of the human will but in real synergy and cooperation with human will and effort. And, precisely because of this doctrine of synergy between grace and freedom, any idea of merit is totally absent from the Orthodox cult and understanding of the Saints. Orthodoxy rejects the formulation of the dogma of Immaculate Conception (although it calls Mary *Immaculate*) precisely because this formulation is in terms of merits and of a "meritorious" doctrine of grace. Asceticism (and that includes every effort, every "good deed") is not guided by any interest in merits. It is man's effort to make himself available for and open to divine grace. It is purification of heart and will so that it may become the abode of the Holy Trinity. "Marvelous is God in his Saints." This liturgical exclamation, which belongs to every service honoring a Saint, expresses well the fundamental character of the cult of Saints, the joyful contemplation of God in the one who has loved him and found in him the fulfillment of his own self.

The Orthodox doctrine of grace, in order to be fully understood, must be considered together with the doctrine of Creation and the doctrine of sin, especially Original Sin.

It is the urgent task for the ecumenical dialogue, it seems to me, to analyze this divergence of approaches between the East and the West. For ultimately we have here two different basic institutions of the fundamental relationship between God and the world, between God and man, and this means, of course, of God himself. Can these two approaches be reconciled? The recent significant developments, such as the revival of biblical theology, the liturgical movement, the new interest in spirituality, seem to indicate the possibility of *rapprochement* or at least of a better understanding of the Eastern position.

The Catholic Tradition

JEAN DANIÉLOU, S.J.

THE CHURCH

I.

The Church is the work of God alone. It is the continuation of the *magnalia Dei* of the Old and New Testaments. It is itself sacred history—sacred history as present. All this is true both of the Church as "spiritual community" and as "visible society" (Vatican II, Constitution on the Church, No. 8).

The Word of God who, with the Spirit, fashioned the first Adam laid hold of the race of Adam once again in the Incarnation and, after having purified it with the blood of his Passion, gave it life by the Resurrection and, by the Ascension, brought it into the Father's house: the Father filled with the Spirit the humanity taken on by the Son. But this vitalization of the humanity of Christ, by which salvation is already substantially achieved, was consummated in him only in order to be communicated to all mankind. This is the pouring forth of the Spirit which began at Pentecost.

The Church is the community of those who have been incorporated into the risen Christ, have been vivified by the Holy Spirit, have become the children of the Father.

The community character of all this is not something secondary. Rather is it constitutive of humanity in God's design. Just as there is a solidarity in sin, so also is there a solidarity in grace (Rom.

5:18) which finds its full expression in the Pauline theology of the "Body of Christ." Of this Body, Christ, the Incarnate Word, exalted in his humanity to the right hand of the Father, is the head. From him comes every grace and spiritual gift. The "seating at the right hand of the Father" designates this particular mystery of Christ, between the Ascension and the *Parousia*, of which we are contemporaries: Christ, the sun of the new creation, vivifies all spiritual beings whether they be on earth or in heaven. Further, according to the teaching of Paul, a solidarity exists as well between the members of the Body which, by their sinfulness or by their sanctity, affects the entire Body: this is the "communion of saints" in which each one cooperates in the Body's growth according to the measure of his activity and his dependence on the head.

The Church is the work of God in its institutional structure as well, a structure which dates back to the public life of Jesus. Jesus consecrated almost all his ministry to the setting up of this structure by his calling of the Twelve, by his making them learn by heart teachings they did not yet understand because the Spirit had not yet been given, in his conferring upon them the power to baptize, to remit sins, to consecrate the bread and wine—power that was to be exercised only when the Spirit had been given. This doctrinal, sacramental, and hierarchic structure, having as its sole object to communicate the life of the risen Christ, could only be put in operation after the Resurrection. That is why it is at Pentecost that the Church began to be a reality.

The Church is concretely revealed under this aspect in the Acts of the Apostles. There the Church is the assemblage of those who have believed and have been baptized. Essentially it is a local Church centered in the Eucharist. It is "the community of saints"—of those, that is to say, who participate in the Sacraments. Under this aspect the Church appears as the unfailing means for the communicating of Revelation and resurrection, unfailing because it is God alone who here works through these human instruments. The Church, again, is the continuation of the mystery of the Covenant according to which God's love, sovereignly and without possibility of recall, spreads abroad God's gifts in giving them to a community which he himself set up. The idea of institution, that is to say, of irrevocable gift, is the equivalent of the biblical notion of covenant. It is under this aspect that the Church is set in relief by the biblical images of Paradise (where the deifying *energeia* are actively present), or of the sheepfold, or of the ship (outside of which no one can survive), or of the temple built of living stones (where alone the sacrifice acceptable to God is offered), or of the espoused to whom God the Spouse has freely and forever given what he himself has in order that she dispose of it as she will.

These dual aspects of the Church, spiritual community and visible society, it is normally impossible to separate wholly from one another. "Visible society" sets in relief the gratuity of one's belonging to the Church because this belonging has its origin in a sacramental action which does not immediately imply one's free cooperation. Thus is it that in a Christian culture Baptism is normally conferred upon everyone, particularly upon infants. It is of the Church's essence that it be "a great multitude" (Rev. 7:9) of the baptized. The Church has always rejected sectarian doctrines which would have it limited to a small witnessing community. From this point of view, the development of the Church in mediaeval and Byzantine civilizations would be the normal thing: the construction of a cadre of Christendom outside of which a Christian people is not possible.

But, on the other hand, the Mystical Body aspect puts emphasis upon the Church as a community of life where each member ought freely to cooperate with the initiating grace given him in Baptism so as to make his own the ways of Christ and be transformed in him. In this sense, life in the Church has a personal character. This cooperating of the person is expressive not only of an exigency in regard to oneself but of a responsibility in regard to the entire Body. It is to the extent that each member is alive and active that the whole Body grows up in charity and matures. One's visible belonging to the Church accordingly implies at the same time a universal vocation to sanctity.

That one preserve, theologically, an equilibrium between these two aspects is essential. To do so is all the more difficult in that a certain marginal zone is, by implication, also present here.

For one thing, the baptized person continues to be a member of the Church as visible society whatever his faults or unfaithfulness. He will never have to be rebaptized: the gift given him remains irrevocably his even if he lets it lie fallow. But he is, at the same time, somehow apart from the spiritual community to the extent that, of this Body, he is a dead member. Further, a person can share in the spiritual life without Baptism and visible membership in the Church. So there is this mysterious twilight zone where the Spirit of God, already present, inwardly solicits hearts in order to draw them to the Church and does so before they have so much as even recognized the Church. However, these two situations, that of the baptized person separated from the spiritual community and that of the person stirred to life previous to Baptism, are limited situations and they ought not to be thought usual.

II.

So far we have described the Church as being, in the limited sense, the community of the baptized. But in the large sense the Church is the community of all the saved, the one destiny (*eschatos*) of mankind in God's design. To say this is, by implication, to say extraordinarily much.

The Church was foreshadowed "from the beginning of the world and, throughout the history of the Israelites under the Old Covenant, marvelously prepared for" (Constitution on the Church, No. 2). The gathering together of the saved at the end of time dominates wholly the transforming of world and time. The transforming, for all of that, is had on successive plateaus. It is for this reason that the time before the Incarnation is to be thought of as a preparation. For society, it is a preparation of a pedagogical sort, as St. Paul suggests (Gal. 3:24), and, after him, St. Irenaeus. For the individual, it is an undoubted pattern of salvation.

The Church "was constituted in the last days and manifested by the effusion of the Spirit" (Constitution on the Church, No. 2). Since then, all men are called to be part of it. It is, since then, the sole pattern of salvation; to say this is to indicate first of all its necessity. It is, since then, the sole way of salvation; Judaism and the pagan religions have become void. There is nothing of the intolerant about this exclusivism of the Church. In consequence of its divine character it is the present locus of sacred history.

A further characteristic is the universality—or catholicity—of the Church. Chiefly, the meaning here is that the Church is not bound up in any single civilization but should express itself through any and all forms of civilization. Although it has to permeate sociological realities, the Church is not itself a sociological reality. The implication here is that the Church is in itself diverse. This it is, not in its constitutive datum, but in the different ways in which the one Gospel is lived by different peoples in diverse cultures. It is the total human realness that the Church, continuing the incarnational program of the Word, would take up in order to consecrate it to the Father. "In virtue of this catholicity, every part gives of its own gifts to other parts and to the Church entire" (Constitution on the Church, No. 13).

The need for the Church and the universality of the Church have as their consequence the missionary character of the Church. At the outset the Apostles were sent to all nations. It is, indeed, through the preaching of the Gospel that men are able to have access to the Church. The total Church is under this obligation to mission. Every baptized person is, by the simple reality of his Baptism, constituted apostle. And to the successors of the Apostles this word and this work have been confided in a particular and privileged fashion. Yet mission is first of all the achievement of the Holy Spirit. In the first age of the Church it was beyond human capabilities quite as it goes beyond them today. That is why the slackening of missionary zeal in the face of difficulties that surround one comes not from such external obstacles but from lack of faith.

The last days have already been inaugurated in the Church. Nevertheless it still remains that this Church, "to which we are all called in Christ and in which we acquire holiness by God's grace, will be brought to completion only in heavenly glory when 'the time for establishing all' (Acts 3:21) will come" (Constitution on the Church, No. 48). The Church accordingly belongs to a kind of intermediary period: "The renewal of the world has already been irrevocably decreed and, here and now, is already in a certain sense anticipated" (*ibid.*). However, "it does not yet appear what we shall be" (1 Jn. 3:2). What is awaited is the cosmic manifestation of what is already hiddenly possessed.

Hence the present earthly Church is a foreshadowing—the foreshadowing of the heavenly Church which is to come. Still in a state of testing and of suffering, it is assailed by forces of evil which, substantially vanquished by Christ, yet make a show of strength.

"Until the day of the 'new heavens and a new earth in which righteousness dwells' (2 Pet. 3:13) the Church is on pilgrimage and bears, in those creatures of this age—its Sacraments and institutions—the form of a world which passes and lives its life amid a creation that 'has been groaning in travail until now' and 'waits with eager longing for the revealing of the sons of God' (Rom. 8:22, 19)" (Constitution on the Church, No. 48).

SCRIPTURE

I.

From the outset Scripture is to be seen as situated within the total pattern of the Christian *oikonomia* because it is a constitutive element of that *oikonomia*. As a matter of fact, the Bible is something quite other than a "sacred book," as that term is used in other religions. The Bible is related to the Christian datum precisely in regard to what is distinctive about that datum.

The subject of Scripture is the history of salvation. For that reason, the primary thing about Scripture is the event and not the word. It is the event which, through the word, is attained. Or, to express it differently, there is no necessity that one be either Jew or Christian in order to know God, while it is necessary to be Jew or Christian in order to believe that God has entered into history, to believe that there are "divine events." The continuity of these divine events makes up the history of salvation. Acts which are properly God's acts—acts of creation, liberation, covenant, presence, judgment—are its content. It is, in the Christian faith, question only of that. And it is only in the Christian faith that it is question of that. The entire cosmic and temporal process is embraced by this history and its profoundest depths are presented there once more because the history of salvation stretches all the way from the creation of the cosmos to the *Parousia*.

This history, further, is eschatological history. In it, unlike in mythology where it is forever question of the recovering of some divine dimension of existence that was had in some pre-existence, it is question of the expectation of God's decision whence salvation will come. In this sense is the Old Testament prophetic, recalling past events as it does in order to stir alive a hope for what God is going to accomplish at the end of time. The New Testament provides witness to a fulfilling of promises: by his Incarnation, his Passion, his Resurrection, Christ is the fulfillment of prophecy because he is himself the eschatological event; he is "the last Adam." That both the Law and the Prophets speak of him is, in this sense, rigorously true.

This eschatological event is everywhere these "last days," as Scripture calls them, these days of the Church when the salvation brought about in the humanity of Christ, who is the head, spreads abroad throughout the Church, which is the body. It should not be thought that here we have something over and above Jesus Christ; rather is it the deployment through space of Jesus Christ.

Here, so far, two aspects: eschatology and event. From even the briefest consideration of them a further (and last) aspect comes to the fore, that of typology. Typology means this: that among the events of the history of salvation in its various stages there exists a meaningful basis of analogy—that of the ways of God—which has set up a distinctive order of reality. It is to it that faith responds.

To believe is always to believe in God's acts—creation, salvation, covenant, which, the *mirabilia Dei*, occur upon graduated levels: there is quite a difference between what happened before Abraham and what happened after him, between what happened before the Incarnation and what happens after it. Within this perspective the Old Testament is a foreshadowing of the New, and the New Testament is, in its turn, a foreshadowing of eternal life. This sort of co-inherence of God's design should be a fundamental consideration in the interpretation of Scripture; the different components of Scripture are not explainable by something external to them; on the contrary, one is explained and justified by another.

II.

The divine events which go to make up the history of salvation are beyond human intelligence so far as their theological content is concerned. In order for them to be known they have to be "unveiled." They have, in short, to be revealed. Happily the one same Word of God brings about the divine events and provides the understanding of them; the Word of God is, at one and the same time, both creative and revelatory. The single, identical Spirit of God brings one to the knowledge of these events by the irresistible power by which the events themselves were brought about: "Only the Spirit of God sounds the depths of God" (Eph. 2:10).

So far as the history of salvation is concerned, Revelation comes second because it is revelation of the history. To put it most simply, God created the cosmos before he revealed that he created the cosmos. Similarly, and less simply, faith in the revelation of the Resurrection of Christ presupposes the historic reality of the Resurrection of Christ. Any minimizing of that historic reality with reference to its revelation tents Scripture itself to the very quick. "If Christ is not risen, preaching is vain, faith is vain" (1 Cor. 15:14).

The revelation of the history of salvation, which of necessity goes hand in hand with the history of salvation, has the same characteristics as the history of salvation itself. It, too, is a divine event. It is a deed of the power of God alone which acquaints man with the mystery of the designs of God by outward manifestation and by inner persuasion—the both at the same time. Revelation and the history of salvation are coextensive: "God who by his Word has created all things, himself at all times giving witness

46

among men by the created universe and by opening up the ways of eternal salvation, was manifested from the very origin of the first human beings. After their fall he raised them up in hope of salvation, promising them liberation and never ceasing to provide for them. He called Abraham in his day . . . And, having spoken in multiple fashions by the Prophets, finally in our day has he spoken in his Son" (Vatican II, Constitution on Divine Revelation, Nos. 3, 4).

Therefore, just as the history of salvation has successive stages, so also does Revelation. And each stage has its distinctive content. There was an initial revelation of God through nature. With the interior suasion of grace, men have been able to recognize God's acting in nature. And God spoke in Old Testament times by the Prophets. His word was addressed to them, letting them know the story of salvation from its origin, letting them recognize his acting in Israel, baring before their eyes the last, the eschatological, events. By the Prophets this revelation was passed on to the People of God who, beneath the ministrations of grace, clung to it in faith. Then, in Jesus Christ, the subsistent Word, the hidden purpose of God was entirely and definitively laid bare. To this revelation nothing could be added. This revelation Christ confided to the Apostles, giving them the ability to express it in its entirety. Lastly, in the time of the Church, the event of the Word, coextensive with the history of salvation, goes on because of the unchanging conservation and the infallible interpretation of the Apostolic revelation in the Apostolic Succession and because of the workings of grace inviting the heart to adhere by faith to that revelation now proffered by the Church.

III.

Scripture is the putting into writing of that word by which the divine content of history was revealed. Scripture, therefore, represents a third stage. The witnesses of the word might also have been the actual human authors of Scripture, but that is not necessarily the case. Abraham and Elijah received Revelation, but they are not the authors of Genesis or the Books of Kings, and Mark and Luke put into writing Revelation that was committed to the Apostles. However, this putting into written form is also a divine event—what we call "inspiration." In this sense Scripture can be called the work of the Holy Spirit. The sacred authors, even as they used their human talents, were aided by the Holy Spirit in such a way that, "as he acted in them and by them, they put into writing all, and only, those things which he himself wished" (*ibid.*, No. 11).

Holy Scripture, thus having behind it the guarantee of divine authority, is a privileged instrument by which we have access to both the history and Revelation. Still, Scripture is not to be substituted for history or for Revelation.

There are, then, three divine realities we are talking about here which should never be separated. To separate Scripture from history is to offer formulas as the object of one's faith instead of events and to make a gnosticism out of Christianity. To separate Scripture from Revelation is to misapprehend the fact that the divine event of Revelation is coextensive with the history of salvation through those to whom Revelation was confided.

The Spirit who inspired Scripture is also the Spirit who continues active in the history of salvation and in the understanding of that history. The Spirit who inspired Scripture is the Spirit who makes possible the interpretation of Scripture in function of an unfolding history of salvation. The Old Testament, which the Church has received as its heritage, is not simply a written text; it is a text as it was interpreted by the People of God. In this regard few things are more remarkable than the liberty enjoyed by the primitive Church, so far as the text of the Old Testament is concerned, as is evidenced by the citations of it in the New Testament and in the Apostolic Fathers. But the New Testament is Scripture in the same fashion; it lives on in the People of God and ought to be interpreted by Tradition for its implications to become clear. To do so has been particularly the work of the councils, from that of Nicaea to that of Vatican II. Scripture is definitive and nothing can be added to it. Yet the Spirit living in the Church and active in the Church unceasingly makes the Church grow in the understanding of Scripture.

The work of the Holy Spirit, Scripture is at the same time the work of the sacred writers; they are "true authors." It is this fact of their authorship which sets up an entire *complexus* of difficulties which hermeneutics seeks to resolve. The books of the Bible came from definite times and milieus and their authors wrote in dependence upon those times and milieus. Especially were they dependent upon the languages they used. But the word of God was not thereby tethered to Hebrew or to Greek. So it is translated, "transferred," into other languages. In short, it is "interpreted." And no one is disturbed. Yet many scholars identify the biblical with the Semitic and therefore see alteration in any effort to de-Semitize. But the need for translating, "transferring," "interpreting," is obvious when it is question of the cosmological, sociological, and cultural representations used in the Bible. To discern what of these representations should be translated and what is the very reality of sacred history is difficult. Many today are tempted to reject the reality (miracles, for instance) as being only representation. The fault here, of course, is the fault of those who first presented as reality what was only representation (for example, in the description of Paradise and of the Fall). Hermeneutics ought always to take account of two criteria, literary criticism on the one hand and the proper content of the history of salvation on the other. It is question here of probing the reality of this history and not of making it vanish.

TRADITION AND TRADITIONS

In the language of Christendom, the word "tradition" has a definite connotation which is not at all the same as what it has in everyday language. There it refers essentially to the temporal: what is traditional is what comes from the past—especially what comes from an extremely remote past. In the Christian vocabulary "tradition" refers to the personal: what is traditional is what had its origin in the person of the Apostles. Thus it is that many traditions which go all the way back to the primitive Church are not part and parcel of Tradition. The primitive Church was a church quite as were the others, so far as its Judaeo-Christian practices and doctrines were concerned.

Here, then, aside from a word or two about traditions, I would speak of tradition in the Christian, the dogmatic sense.

I.

That there was tradition, the passing on by the Apostles of the teaching, of the institutions, and of the witness to events concerning Christ, is incontestable. Christ confided the riches of his truth and of his life to the Apostles while promising them the aid of the Holy Spirit. And this deposit which was confided to them, the Apostles faithfully passed on. An initial datum, accordingly, is certain: the priority in time of Tradition over Scripture and, on the other hand, the priority in time of the divine institution over Tradition. Tradition, like the Sacraments, is an aspect of the Church. Like the Church itself, Tradition is a means established by Christ in order to communicate his saving work to men to the end of time. Tradition is an act of the Holy Spirit. It is a form of the Covenant.

What the Apostles received was written down by themselves or by others of the Apostolic Age under the inspiration of the Holy Spirit. That is what goes to make up the Scripture of the New Testament. But this writing down of the Apostolic Tradition did not do away with the prior institution of oral tradition through the Apostles and through their successors, the bishops. To this fact the earliest Church writers stand as witnesses. The *Didache*, the *Epistle of Barnabas*, the *Epistle of the Apostles* in their catechetical teaching transmit the tradition of the Faith in a way that is independent of Scripture. The rule of faith, or creed, already attested to by the writings of the New Testament, is the expression of this tradition. St. Irenaeus set this role of Tradition in sharp relief at the end of the second century as he stressed the succession

50

(*diadoche*) of the local churches. "The Faith is the faith received from the Fathers," Gregory of Nyssa will say later. Irenaeus even declares that, if all the Scriptures were to disappear, the integrity of the Faith would be guaranteed by Tradition.

Because of data of this sort, it is possible to bring the nature of Tradition into clearer focus.

On the one hand, Tradition does not trespass upon what remains the prerogative of the Apostles, that is, to be source of Revelation. Apostolic in its source, it is ecclesiastical in its transmission. It is, accordingly, only a form of transmission. But it alone has normative value. Pure church tradition, as are certain practices, is worthy of respect but it is not clothed in the same authority. Here, then, is what marks off the boundaries of Tradition and prevents its intruding into the domain of Revelation.

But, on the other hand, Tradition is not merely the continuation of the Apostles' teaching as operative throughout the Christian community. It has a norm that is invested with special authority: the hierarchy, heirs of the Apostles to whom Revelation was confided in a particular way. The authority of the hierarchy, as it is expressed in dogmatic definitions, is guaranteed by the assistance of the Holy Spirit. To say this is to say that it is protected from error. And this is what goes to make up the present form of the Spirit's activity in the Church—an activity which is in continuity with that of the Spirit in the people of Israel and in the Apostles. The hierarchy, accordingly, have, in the transmission of Revelation, an authority equal to that of the Apostles in the communication of Revelation.

II.

The content of Tradition is Revelation as communicated by the Apostles. The content of the New Testament scriptures is, in the same way, Revelation. Tradition and Scripture have the same content. Revelation is one. Its way of coming to us is double. Tradition is the transmission of Revelation by a channel different from Scripture, that is, by the teaching of the Church. But this is an aspect of no real importance because it seems there is nothing in Tradition which is not, in some fashion, contained in Scripture as well. It is in regard to institutions rather than doctrines that the question can come up. Sacraments are an example. Yet even with Sacraments it is not certain that there are constitutive elements of their divine institution which are attested only in Tradition. When St. Basil speaks of traditions coming from the Apostles he enumerates praying toward the East and standing when one prays during the Pentecostal season, practices which doubtless go back to the Apostles but are only traditions. Scripture is the usual criterion by which it is determined whether a doctrine pertains to the Faith or not.

So the importance of Tradition does not consist in its being a source distinct from Scripture but in its being an authority by which it becomes possible to interpret what is the common content of Scripture and Tradition. Such was the interpretation of the Old Testament by the New. For primitive Christianity the Gospel was the authentic explanation of the Old Testament, an explanation after the fashion of the Jewish *pesher*. The New Testament scriptures have preserved examples of this exegesis, as the application, for instance, to Christ of the prophecies concerning the rock or the lamb. This Christological exegesis of the Old Testament was an authoritative exegesis and has continued to be that in Tradition. Rightly did Origen make spiritual (that is, typological) exegesis one of the elements of the common Faith, because it is an exegesis not of the scientific sort; it is an expression of faith.

On the other hand, one of the characteristics of Revelation is that it is centered essentially upon events, whether it is question of the Gospels or of the Creed. Now affirmations are implicit in these events—affirmations which, by unavoidable necessity, have to be made explicit, for pure biblicism is an impossibility. The trouble is in coming to exact expression, a consummation achieved only little by little. Thus the New Testament puts us in the presence of the Father and of the Son and of the Spirit as three indubitable facts. It does not, however, explain the relations between them. Three centuries were necessary in order to come to the point of giving an exact expression to the relations. Today, whether we be Catholic,

Orthodox, or Protestant, we read the New Testament in the light of the Councils of Nicaea and Chalcedon; to refuse to do so would be to condemn oneself to going over once again the long distance from adoptionism or subordinationism to consubstantialism. The definitions of the Immaculate Conception or of the infallibility of the bishop of Rome derive from that same necessity: they are exact formulations of data implicit in Scripture.

Revelation does not increase, but the understanding of Revelation does increase continuously. And the increase is brought about under the influence of the Holy Spirit. As I have remarked before, it is the same Spirit who inspired Scripture and Tradition that provides one's understanding of them. And he provides this understanding through the same organs by which he made its transmission certain so that this understanding, which comes from him, is a sure and infallible understanding.

This understanding is the understanding of the Church entire: "Living tradition develops in the Church with the assistance of the Holy Spirit. Undertanding of the realities as much as of the words transmitted grows in the contemplation of the faithful and their intimate experience of spiritual things." But "the mission of authentically interpreting the word of God, whether it be written or handed down, was confided solely to the living magisterium of the Church" (Vatican II, Constitution on Divine Revelation, Nos. 8 and 10).

III.

A distinction is necessary between Tradition in the dogmatic sense of the word, that which has to do with the unerring handing down and the authentic explaining of revealed datum, and "traditions," an entire range of practices—or doctrines—which go back to early Christianity or at least to the first Christian centuries and yet are not part of the deposit confided by Christ to the Apostles.

It was never an easy matter to distinguish between the two and it is not easy to do so today. Clement of Alexandria, for instance, called tradition (and linked to the oral teaching of the Apostles) a congeries of speculations about the sacred cosmos which today we know were bits and pieces of Judaeo-Christian theology. It is possible that they dated from Apostolic times. It is also possible that they were elaborated by the Apostles. But they are not part of the revealed deposit. The New Testament provides traces of them in certain Johannine or Pauline speculations which come from the *genre littéraire* of apocalyptic. St. Justin included millenarianism among traditional doctrines. The same holds for numerous rites which go back to the original Judaeo-Christian milieu and are part and parcel of the incarnation of Christianity in the Jewish milieu. But they are not part and parcel of its revealed content.

Thus, in the course of its history, Christianity developed a complete liturgical cycle: the daily, the weekly, the yearly. Thus the Holy Spirit raised up saints who in each of their epochs enriched the spiritual tradition of the Church. Thus the great Doctors and Fathers of the Church deepened innumerable aspects of the Christian mystery. All this sort of thing goes to make up an infinitely precious treasure and source by which the Faith is attested.

The word of God, however, is not so bound that it cannot be expressed in new forms, and there is a danger of ancient traditions smothering living Tradition. So the importance of these developments must be properly understood. To do so is not a matter of going back to their origins, for, as we have said, ancientness as such is no guarantee of truth. Apostolicity alone is that. The solitary norm is precisely the revealed deposit itself handed down in a living fashion in the Church and capable of being expressed in different fashions according to differing times and regions. It is question of distinguishing what is irreformable, that is, Tradition, and that which ought to be ceaselessly reformed, that is, the traditions. And there only the authority of the Church is able to intervene.

The Church is above the cult of either the traditional or of the avant-garde. What the Church calls Tradition in no wise accords the past a position of privilege. Nothing would be more contrary to the prophetic and eschatological attitude characteristic of Judaeo-Christianity in contrast to pagan religions than this would be. For

Judaeo-Christianity, history has a positive content and is marked by irreversible development. But, on the other hand, Christianity does not expect the solution of the problems of human destiny to come from time. It does not exalt the future any more than it does the past. Indeed, for it, the essential event has already happened in the Resurrection of Jesus Christ, the decisive eschatological event beyond which there is nothing. Thus the Christian position is irreducible to the systems in which one might wish to enclose it.

The authentic notion of Tradition is precisely the expression of this original attitude.

SACRAMENTS

In the ancient tradition the explanation of the Sacraments was wholly founded upon the analogy of the Sacraments and the *mirabilia Dei* in the Old Testament. At first glance we are brought up short by the seemingly arbitrary character of such correlations as these. To have Baptism correlated with the Flood or with the passage through the Red Sea because Baptism is conferred with water and water plays a role in each of these episodes, leaves us puzzled. Actually, however, what the Fathers of the Church emphasize is not first of all the analogy of the signs but that of the realities. Let us take St. Ambrose: "That there was in the Red Sea a figure of this Baptism, the Apostle himself says: 'Our fathers were baptized in the cloud and in the sea.' And he adds: 'All this was done for them in figure.' When Moses lifted up his rod the Jewish people had been cut off in every direction. The Egyptian was on the one side with his army and on the other side the Hebrews were stopped by the sea" (*De Sacramentis*, I, 19).

Thus what St. Ambrose insists upon is that the essential thing is a particular situation. The significance of the passage through the Red Sea is that it expresses a desperate state, one without human solution. It was only by the intervention of God that the people were delivered. But the situation of a catechumen at the side of the baptismal font is the same: he is in that desperate situation par excellence which is spiritual death and bodily mortality. The same

55

holds for the other figures of Baptism. Comparison is made between the water of Baptism and the primeval waters upon which the Spirit of God moved: the essential thing here is first of all that only the Spirit of God brought about the initial creation; by this correlation Baptism is shown us as a new creation. Comparison is made with the waters of the Flood: the world was in sin; the judgment of God struck the sinful world: the essential thing here is that Baptism appears as a judgment of God which destroys sinful man: "You have been buried with Christ by Baptism."

True of Baptism, all this is true also of the other Sacraments. Let us take the Eucharist. We say in the words of consecration: "This is my blood, the blood of the New Covenant, which will be shed for you unto the remission of sins." The text is compact with biblical references. But here again we must go beyond the analogy of the signs to that of the realities: Moses had poured blood on the people and on the altar; and that division of blood signified the Covenant, that is to say, the sharing in a life definitively brought into existence: "They will be my people and I will be their God." The Eucharist is covenant. Yahweh had directed the blow of his anger onto his enemies; the blood of Christ is poured out, in blessing now and not in malediction, for at least those who do not drink their own damnation.

Yahweh dwelt in the Temple of Jerusalem. This dwelling, this presence, has been one of the distinctive characteristics of sacred history. But in the Eucharist, the Word of God dwells in the new Temple which is the Church made of living stones. It is in the new Temple that the new priesthood, the royal priesthood, of which the First Epistle of Peter speaks, offers up spiritual sacrifices, that is to say, the sacrifices of the man renewed by the Spirit and which are acceptable to the Father. The blood of the paschal lamb, put on the doors of the Egyptian homes, turned the avenging angel aside. Thus the judgment of God should strike every sinner, but his judgment passes over (*pesha*) and spares those who are marked with the blood of the lamb, those who have borne the weight of his anger—although they were innocent—in order that this weight might weigh no longer on those who were sinners.

We have been emphasizing so far the analogies that exist between the *mirabilia Dei* of the Old Testament and the Sacraments. It is clear, however, that the New Testament is situated in the same perspective. It is by analogy with the Old Testament that the New Testament allows us to understand the theological content of the actions of Christ: he is the new creature whom the Spirit raises up in the womb of Mary; his humanity is the Temple where the Son of God has set up his abode; he is covenant, not only the New Covenant, but the Everlasting Covenant because the life of God was given completely and definitively to humanity. And the Sacraments, in turn, refer to these mysteries: Baptism is an imitation of the death of Christ which produced its real effect; it is an imitation of the Resurrection of Christ which produced its real effect; it is a sharing in the Covenant concluded in Christ; it is a participation in the judgment accomplished in Christ; it is a sharing in the presence realized in Christ.

We come then to this conclusion: the relation established by the patristic catechesis between Sacraments and acts of God in the Old and New Testaments signifies that the Sacraments correspond to situations which are discoverable on various levels of the history of salvation. Divine, they occur within an area of existence which is neither that of eternal perfections nor that of eternal relations. The area, rather, is that of God's interventions in history. But these interventions of God in history are properly the object of Faith. To lay bare this core in the Sacraments is accordingly to attain to the very substance of the Sacraments. So a definition which basically I borrow from Oscar Cullmann: "The Sacraments are the continuation in the time of the Church of the great acts of God in the Old and New Testaments."

Some important conclusions from all this: We are able to arrive at what constitutes the essential core of the Sacraments. More than that, the very relation established between them and God's actions throughout the two Testaments has consequences. It shows the Sacraments to be part of sacred history and it makes clear that sacred history lives on not just in books but in reality. It grounds faith in the Sacraments upon Faith in the acts of God among his people of old and, these last days, in Christ. (This is what the archangel Gabriel did when he provided Mary the analogy of what God had accomplished in Elizabeth in order to give basis to her own act of Faith.) The act of Faith is not of faith in the arbitrary or in the absurd but, on the contrary, in the continuity of a design that gives it intelligibility and locates its purpose and makes it thinkable.

Finally, this analogy clarifies the content of the Sacraments, showing us that their content is in no way different from the other ways of God's acting for his ways of acting are always the same. It is possible to summarize them: at all the levels of the history of salvation, God creates, God saves, God is present, God judges, God makes covenant. And Faith is to believe this whether it be in the Old Testament, in Christ, or in the Sacraments.

This analogy contributes a wonderful simplification to religious teaching in freeing it from the disparate. Whether it is question of exegesis or of spirituality or of theology or of morals, it is always the same thing that is in question. A unifying of Christian knowledge is thus possible. And it is surely more worthwhile to spend one's time in the effort to understand what are the ways of God, to aid the act of Faith in the acts of God, than to scatter one's attention abroad through the secondary questions.

So far we have tried to point out that sacramental acts are the same as God's acts among his people of old and in Christ. But, if these are the same, they are also different because they are situated in different moments of the history of salvation and it is not question here simply of God's intervention but of interventions *as present.* Typology is an analogy of God's ways at various stages of sacred history, and as soon as you say analogy you say sameness and difference. Accordingly, we must now situate these particular forms of creation, of presence, of salvation, of covenant, of judgment which are the Sacraments.

That the Old Testament, Christ, the Sacraments, present distinct contents is surely clear. But what is the character of this present time which is the time of the Church? First of all, it is subsequent to the essential event of sacred history which substantially attained its end in the Incarnation and the Resurrection. Humanity has been saved and the glory of God has been achieved. There cannot henceforth be another such event. Yet what was accomplished in the humanity of Christ is to be communicated to all mankind. Glorified and seated at the right hand of the Father, Christ now builds his Body which is the Church. It is this mystery of Christ which fills the space of time that extends from the Ascension to the *Parousia*. It is Christ, thus in glory, who fills it entirely. It has no other content nor can it have. The sacramental structure is in correspondence with this character of the present moment in sacred history.

But, on the other hand, what was accomplished in Christ is not yet apparent. The second characteristic of the sacramental structure of the history of salvation is then a certain hiddenness: "You are dead and your life is hidden with Christ in God. When Christ your life will appear then will you appear also in his glory" (Col. 3:3-4). The sacramental acts are in accord with an epoch of the history of salvation when the eschatological reality has already been accomplished but is not yet manifest: "You are already sons of God but what you will be one day is not yet manifest" (1 Jn. 3:2). Or again: "All creation groans awaiting the manifestation of the sons of God" (Rom. 8:22). The divine filiation is already accomplished but—except in Mary—its total appearing remains in suspense.

Such is the epoch of sacred history in which we live and it corresponds to a mystery of Christ. The last of the past mysteries is the mystery of the Ascension. The future mystery is the mystery of the *Parousia*. The only mystery which is in the present is Christ's sitting at the right hand of the Father—the mystery of him, exalted in the glory of the Father, who builds up his own Body until having put all his enemies beneath his feet (that is to say, having established the reign of God in every creature), he restores all things to his Father offering him the achieved creation as a sacrifice of eternal praise for all eternity amid the marveling of the angels. The Sacraments correspond to this progressive consecration of man and of the universe. They have their *locus* in the hidden universe of the heart. It is only when the reign of God will have been established in all hearts that he will manifest himself in the body: *futurae gloriae nobis pignus*.

Finally, I would like to indicate how this interpretation of the

59

Sacraments as events in the history of salvation allows one to resolve a difficulty encountered in the administering of the Sacraments. The difficulty is this: the sacramental rites are no longer intelligible to the man of today. The reason is that modern man has lost his sense of the symbolic dimension of cosmic and natural realities. Water and fire, bread and wine, oil and salt had a sacral meaning for ancient man. They do not have it for the man of today. The world, for him, is de-sacralized. I do not here pose the question of whether this is a temporary malaise or a permanent stage. I merely state the fact. But the point to be kept in mind is that the symbolism of the Sacraments is not based on analogies drawn from the cosmos. It is not question of the natural symbolism of water or of wine, of oil or of salt. At most, such symbolism is secondary. Rather is it a question before all else of the analogy between historic situations, that is to say, between essentially human realities. And the man of today is precisely of a particular sensitiveness regarding human realities. Situations such as captivity and deliverance, solitude and society, condemnation and acquittal, presence and absence, confidence and its lack, are all too familiar to him.

GRACE

I.

The anthropology of the New Testament contains elements borrowed from Semitic culture which are no more a part of revelation as such than were the elements borrowed from Hellenic culture that are to be found in the anthropology of the Fathers. I mean, of course, the entire domain of the soul-body relationship. All too often in this matter is biblical anthropology confused with Semitic anthropology. But Christian anthropology is not concerned with the make-up of man. Instead it concentrates upon the distinction between two states of the human condition. These two states, particularly in the Pauline letters, are designated by terms which stand in mutual opposition, the chief among them being "death" and "life," "flesh" and "spirit," "sin" and "justice." All of them refer to what is the proper object of the Gospel message: the eschatological divine act by which the Word laid hold of human nature in the Incarnation and, after having slain its mortality by the Passion, gave it life from his own divine life at the Resurrection and, at the Ascension, brought it into the sphere of the Trinity.

Life, spirit, justice—all of it is never anything other than a sharing in what was first of all achieved in the humanity of the Son. If this life is particularly called spirit, it is because it is the work of the Holy Spirit, which is to say that it is a life completely beyond the capabilities of man to attain, that it originates in the irresistible power of God alone. The act by which the divine Persons achieved in Christ the salvation of human nature is the eschatological act, the final term of God's design. It is at one and the same time creation, liberation, presence, covenant. In that eschatological act all these expressions find their fullness of meaning.

Man attains to it by faith in it. He attains its effectiveness by Baptism, for Baptism is, according to the words of St. Basil, "a ritual imitation of the Passion, of the Resurrection, and of the Ascension that brings about their real effect." It is divine act as present; it is the event of sacred history as present. The baptized person is a new creature "born of water and the Spirit"; he has passed from death to life; he is the abiding place of the Spirit; the blood of the New Covenant is, in the Eucharist, the effective sign of his communion with the divine Persons. Baptized in the name of the Father and of the Son and of the Holy Spirit, he has received the spirit of the Son in whom he is able to say *Abba, Pater.*

"Life" and "death" here stand for realities that have no relationship to what the same words mean in ordinary speech. "Life" and "death" are here opposed to one another as two spheres of existence, light and darkness. The living are those who live the life of the Spirit. They are, principally, the saints in heaven, who, with

61

THE CONVERGENCE OF TRADITIONS

those upon earth, make up the communion of saints. The dead are those who do not share in this life. The actual boundaries of the two spheres are known to God alone.

Admittedly, the biblical metaphors get mixed, but the essential doctrinal drift is clear: The Lamb immolated and exalted at the right hand of the Father is the life-giving sun of this new creation. The Spirit is the river of living water which flows forth from the throne of God and of the Lamb and brings into existence in the holy city, which is the city of the living, the trees of life which are the saints. This grace-created life spreads abroad from the resurrected Christ. It encounters men in their souls by Baptism. It will complete this encounter in their bodies by the resurrection. But from the first to the second there is a mysterious development which our categories of life and death know nothing of. This grace-created life is also the principle of growth in the Body of Christ by which Christ himself builds up his Body through the instrumentality of the Church as he adds new members to it. This missionary dynamism by which the Spirit, who fills the universe, seeks to give life to all is a constitutive aspect of grace.

II.

The word "grace" does not denote merely the sphere of spiritual existence. It means as well the access to this sphere which is accorded by the initiative, completely gratuitous, of God's love. This holds true on two levels. First of all, Judaeo-Christianity excludes all that is pantheistic, all that would in any way imply that the divine and the human are homogeneous so that deification would be achieved by asceticism, as it is asserted to be in Neoplatonism, Hinduism, Hegelianism. In Judaeo-Christianity, transcendence means that the abyss which separates God from man is unbridgeable by man. It can be bridged by God and has effectively been bridged by the Word of God. And here we come up against the mystery of the *katabasis*: "No one has ever seen God; the only Son, who is in the bosom of the Father, he has made him known" (Jn. 1:18). All of Christianity is in the two paradoxes that God becomes man (the descent of God) and that man is made God (the Ascension of Christ).

Historically, however, from the very time he first began to exist, man was oriented toward this spiritual existence. He was at the beginning introduced into Paradise, which means into the sphere of spiritual existence. But in reality, outside of Christ, his situation is one of spiritual death. This is what is called "Original Sin" in Western theology, both Catholic and Protestant. To determine the source of this spiritual death is one of the most difficult problems in theology. But all theologies affirm the reality of the state itself. Any minimizing of Original Sin empties the redemptive act of meaning: were man not captive of the powers of evil, Christ would not have had to die in order to destroy upon the Cross the bond which rendered us Satan's captives (cf. Col. 2:14). Grace wells up within a humanity which was entirely hedged in by sin, that is to say, was spiritually dead.

Grace is an absolute beginning: it is prefaced by no human act of good will.

But, if the acquiring of grace does not depend in any way upon man, the losing of grace does depend upon him.

God does not have second thoughts about his gifts: that is the basic principle of the theology of the Covenant. Once given by God in a completely gratuitous act, grace is really possessed by man—not as something that he holds of himself but as a gift that has really been bestowed. This is true of every aspect of the Christian mystery. The Covenant, achieved in Jesus Christ, between the Person of the Son of God and human nature has been effected once for all (*hapax*). The Covenant, by which Christ gave of his own possessions to his Bride the Church so that she might dispose of them as she would, was a covenant effected once for all. Similarly, the gift of grace by Christ in Baptism is given once for all; that is why Baptism cannot be conferred more than once. Again, the body of the Christian is the temple of the Holy Spirit. All these biblical expressions indicate continuity. The "institutional" aspect is therefore as much of a piece with God's way of acting as is the "event" aspect.

Because grace is accorded in a genuine and abiding fashion, it

63

has what characterizes all life, fecundity. Fecundity is what, in a different vocabulary, is intended by the term "merit": the super-abundance of God's giving which brings it about that the justified man is not only made good but is made capable of being a source of good: "He who believes in me, as the Scripture has said, out of his heart shall flow rivers of living water" (Jn. 7:38). So it is that in the Body of Christ each member, under the influence of the head who is Christ, really cooperates in the building up of the Body: "I appointed you that you should go and bear fruit and that your fruit should abide; so that whatever you ask the Father in my name, he may give it to you" (Jn. 15:16). In the natural order the divine causality does not suppress liberty; comparably the universal causality of Christ in the supernatural order does not eliminate the activity of charity.

III.

The humanity which the Word of God assumed in the Incarnation is the same humanity that was created in the beginning. What the Word saved is what was first of all created. And all that has been created is called to be saved.

Here, of course, the problem of the status of earthly values in Christian anthropology presents itself—of the value of intelligence or of human love or of religious experience or of moral experience, of the value of work or of temporal action in general. There is no question of their being in any way proportionate to salvation. Indeed they are completely out of proportion. When in fact they are taken up by men as ends in themselves, they wear the very visage of sin and end up idols. On the other hand, earthly values are in no wise strangers to grace since they are precisely what grace takes up, purifies, and transforms. So there are two dangers to be avoided here: the danger of minimizing them and the danger of exaggerating them. Thus, today, is understanding unduly minimized and the relation to one's neighbor unduly exalted.

A number of questions now come up.

One is the question of natural religion. Clearly unable to achieve salvation, natural religion has always been more or less perverted into idolatry. Yet it is a dimension of man; this is the reason that atheism is radically inhuman. Grace comes to save every man and, therefore, man as religious. Hence the religious values of humanity are not destroyed but are taken up, purified, and transformed by grace. This is a point that seems important in regard to several other matters. Thus from the missionary point of view the one unique Faith should take on different expressions according to the religious genius of different peoples, for what we are inclined to call "Christianity" is in fact Western Christianity, its dogmatic conflicts included. This point, again, is important for the problem of mysticism: mysticism is a reality of the religious man in general but it should be taken up into the life of grace.

Another question is that of the value of intelligence, particularly of its ability to know God. Here again, without revelation, the reasoning effort never comes completely to term. Yet it is nonetheless true that intelligence, even wounded by sin, is able to grasp the real. And intelligence, cured by grace, can know the existence and the attributes of God. So the God of reason is not an idol; it is God imperfectly, yet really, known. One of the dangers today is a putting in question of the metaphysical value of intelligence, a procedure which ends up in skepticism, in subjectivism, in positivism. But the credulity of Christians is in part responsible for this degradation. In any case it is contrary to the doctrine of the basic goodness of creation expressed by the early Christian Doctors in their writings against the heresy of Gnosticism.

A third question is that of a natural law written within the heart of every man and expressive of the dependence of each individual and of the social order itself upon the law of God. It is this which is put in question by the asserting of a complete autonomy in the temporal order. The devastating consequences are apparent today in Continental Liberalism quite as in Communism, for both come from the same source. A contributing factor has been the tendency of Christians to separate the domain of Faith, which concerns only the eternal destiny of persons, from the domain of the earthly city,

65

where man would be fully autonomous. All this is counter to the doctrine of there being a natural morality, individual and social, which grace comes to complete but which first of all it presupposes. Thought upon this makes manifest at one and the same time the distinction of the natural order from the supernatural and their radical interdependence.

The Protestant Tradition

HEIKO A. OBERMAN

INTRODUCTORY: A TALE OF TWO CITIES

One of the oldest endowed lectureships at Harvard University is the Dudleian Lecture, established by Chief Justice Paul Dudley in 1751. According to the statutes it is to be given every fourth year "for detecting and convicting and exposing the idolatry of the Romish Church, their tyranny, usurpations, damnable heresies, fatal errors, abominable superstitions and other crying wickednesses in their high places; and finally, that the Church of Rome is that mystical Babylon, that man of sin, that apostate Church, spoken of in the New Testament."

The spirit of Pope John XXIII has unleased within the Roman Catholic Church a longing for renewal and ecumenicity which had for some time inspired individual theologians and churchmen but can now start to shape and reshape the Roman Catholic Church as such. This is, of course, a matter of great encouragement for the non-Roman brethren in East and West. For those who stand in the Reformation tradition, however, it is more than a sign of the ongoing care of God for his Church and the abiding power of the *Spiritus Creator*. For them it is also a unique opportunity to terminate the Western confessional war of attrition, a chance to recapture the catholicity of the Reformation.

Modern histories—perhaps ecumenically motivated—often tend to present the sixteenth-century debates as marred by bitterness, vitiated by political hunger for power, or determined by simple economic motives. Actually, a closer study of the era is rewarded by the discovery of the depth and reach of the discussions, particularly in the first four decades of this century of upheaval and schism. The Reformers, seen in their own context, prove to have been Doctors acting in responsibility to the whole Catholic Church, sharing in the search for the *ecclesia catholica reformata*. It was in the subsequent centuries of hate, persecution, in-group propaganda and suspicion—in short in a four-century-long cold war—that the points of difference established in the sixteenth-century hot war were extended to many other areas of Christian life and thought, areas where the first generation of Reformers and Counter Reformers had still been able to presuppose a basic unity of devotion and conviction.

This meant for Protestantism an emotional and doctrinal shift from the earlier antipapalism to subsequent antipapism; in the protestant understanding of the task of the Reformers, a shift from their office of Catholic Doctors to pioneers and founders of denominations; and—most disastrously with regard to the purpose of the Reformation—a shift from the vision of an *ecclesia catholica reformata* to an *ecclesia reformata* "tout court." The eighteenth-century formulation of the statutes of Harvard's Dudleian Lectureship is an eloquent example of this cold-war spirituality. Because of the dangerous attrition incurred in this cold war the renewal of Roman Catholicism is at once a challenge and a stimulus for world Protestantism to repossess the catholicity of the Reformation. The possibility and first signs of the end of the Counter Reformation within Roman Catholicism may prove to be the decisive turn in sparking the Protestant quest for a New Reformation.

Protestantism is at the moment in a stage of transition and reorientation which can perhaps best be described as "A Tale of Two Cities." Two orientation points will be of central importance for Protestantism as it reads the map of our time and sets the course for the future: "Vatican City" and the "Secular City."

"Vatican City" suggests of course the wider domain of Roman Catholicism but it is a deliberate choice in that it is an ambiguous symbol both of genuine *Catholicity* within Roman Catholicism and typically *Roman* developments. On the one hand, the recovery of the Catholicity of the Reformation will establish new avenues of communication with the Roman Catholic Church, with the promise of an enrichment of both traditions. On the other hand, "Vatican City" will remain the shorthand for such aspects as Roman political aspirations, papal supremacy, and triumphalistic tendencies within Roman Catholicism to which the Reformation cannot possibly assign a place in an authentic *ecclesia catholica reformata*.

The "Secular City" is a second central but equally ambiguous point of orientation. Christianity all over the world will have to come to terms with secularization, but Protestantism with its agrarian rootage faces a doubly difficult task in coming to terms with the combination of secularization with urbanization. As the book of Professor Harvey Cox, *The Secular City*, makes abundantly clear,[1] this is not just a sociological development which influences only those "secular" structures of the society to which the Church directs the Gospel; it affects the very capacity to hear the Gospel. The "Secular City" is a second ambiguous point of reference insofar as the secular presuppositions require the Church to translate the Gospel into action and thought, to abandon its guerrilla action against the secular revolution and investigate how it can participate in secularization, described as "the loosing of the world from religious and quasi-religious understandings of itself, the dispelling of all closed world-views, the breaking of all supernatural myths and sacred symbols." [2] At the same time this cannot be an unbridled participation, since the capacity to hear the Gospel cannot be allowed to become the standard of the content and validity of the Gospel itself. Against such an experience-oriented theology the words of St. Paul warn us: "As God in his wisdom ordained, the world failed to find him by its wisdom, and he chose to save those who have faith by the folly of the Gospel." [3] A truly Catholic theology is executed in *obedience* to Holy Scripture, in *communion* with the Fathers and *responsibility* for the

[1] New York, 1965; esp. pp. 114 sqq.
[2] Cox's definition of secularization, *op. cit.*, p. 2.
[3] 1 Cor. 1:21 (The New English Bible).

69

brethren. The co-inherence of these three elements should guide us in speaking to the conditions of this age without being conditioned by this age.

This introduction would be more than incomplete if we did not mention that a third city will prove to be of equal relevance as the two mentioned before: Byzantium, or Constantinople. In the West we have developed more experience than expectation in centuries of theological dialogue, debate, and battle. On a number of points we have become so monomaniacal that we tend to lose sight of the wider horizon of the Church of Christ in the Near and Far East. The Reformation was undertaken to reform the Western Church; it drew on certain of the Eastern Fathers, but was by no means intimately exposed to the Eastern Tradition which had become marginal to the Western Church in the Middle Ages.

Without any doubt, the addition of a third partner in the Rome-Reformation encounter complicates our quest considerably. But it can at the same time free us from Western idiosyncrasies which have been obstacles in establishing the unity we have and show us ways to extend the scope of the unity we seek. Though my position papers may still show the after-effects of Western provincialism, they are intended to contribute to a development from dialogue to a triangular comprehension of the mission and message of the Church in our time.

Since the relation of the peoples of the Old Covenant and the New Covenant is a crucial theme running throughout all five of my papers, it is appropriate to conclude these introductory remarks with a quotation from the Psalms:

If I forget you, O Jerusalem, let my right hand wither; let my tongue cleave to the roof of my mouth, if I do not remember you. (Psalm 137: 5–6)

What began as "A Tale of Two Cities" is to be enlarged to contain, together with Vatican City and the Secular City, Constantinople and Jerusalem to provide Protestantism with the necessary orientation in its search to repossess and unfold the Catholicity of the Reformation.

The Church

I.

It has been argued that Christianity broke through the mythological barrier of a Greek philosophical understanding of time by which history is devaluated to a meaningless repetition of periods and seasons, thus becoming an evil trap in which mankind is caught. There is indeed good evidence to show that, in the biblical view, history is purposeful—that it is not a trap out of which man has to be redeemed but the scene and context of redemption. But no one familiar with the Greek philosophical traditions, and especially with the philosophical presuppositions of the Greek and Roman historians before and around the beginning of the Common Era, would be willing to subscribe fully to such a sweeping statement. Yet it is clear that within the Christian Church these two views have confronted each other from the very beginning.

In his first letter to the Corinthians, Chapter 15, St. Paul deals with opponents best designated as gnostics who deny that the resurrection is still to take place. They are the first proponents of what Luther was to call *theologia gloriae*, whose presupposition is a spiritual immediacy to God that is no longer threatened by the powers of this world, no more subject to sin and death. On the other hand, St. Paul's message, based upon "Christ, and him crucified," is clearly future-oriented: enjoying now the *first* gifts of the Spirit, one looks towards Christ's coming in glory and towards the time that God will be "all in all." In the Gospels, Christ's promise of the abiding assistance and guidance of the Holy Spirit constitutes the Apostolic Church as an eschatological community, "in between the times." The Spirit as the Life-saver is to prove more powerful than the gates of hell. This promise can only be understood in the context of the biblical *dualistic* tendency to describe the diabolic powers so realistically that the concept of God's sovereignty is taxed to the limit.[1] In contrast we find a

[1] Heiko Miskotte comments upon Isaiah 45:6, "There is none besides me," with the profound words: "This 'none' is by no means a metaphysical denial,

monistic thrust in Eastern theology in its use of the philosophical concept of *to hon* (being) for God; and more explicitly in Western theology in Augustine's interpretation of Cicero's *Hortensius,* Anselm's *Why Has God Become Man?*, Thomas's doctrine of God as pure act, Cusa's *coincidentia oppositorum,* and, in our time, Paul Tillich's God as "ground of being."

In our time this all-encompassing being—omnipotent, omniscient, omnipresent—is proclaimed dead. He who died, however, is the God of the philosophers, not the God of the Scriptures. The God of the Scriptures is also omnipotent but his is an "omnipotence of survival." His omnipotence is eschatological, hidden, seen in glimpses and only in Faith. According to the theological dualism of the Scriptures, sovereignty is not an immutable property of God in his aseity or an unassailable quality of his being. According to the Scriptures of the two Testaments it is touch-and-go with God's sovereignty. Leaving the Armageddon to sectarian speculation about the termination of history, monistic philosophical theology is unable to cope with the biblical God who is in need of a continuous reassertion that he alone is God. The history of God with his rebellious creation is a battle scene where victory is in abeyance, an ambiguous situation, by Roman historians appropriately referred to as *"ancipiti Marte pugnare."*

Exactly in a time when Origen's star is rising it might be well to remind ourselves that the allegorical method (so masterfully applied by this eminent Alexandrian theologian) was born of the effort to neutralize the anthropomorphic passages in the Old Testament which were unacceptable in a Greek Hellenistic climate determined by monistic philosophies. A God who acts in history and shows regret, wrath, and joy cannot easily be reconciled with *to hon,* with eternal being, with a serene God detached from the ambiguities of history. But the climax of this very same anthropomorphic theology of the Old Testament is the New Testament message that the creator and Lord of history has become flesh to reassert his claims. His paradoxical seizure of power

---

rather a theological one" (my own translation). *Als de Goden zwijgen over de zin van het Oude Testament* (Amsterdam, 1956), blz. 179.

through crucifixion and death, finally, reveals that the mode of the Kingdom of God is incompatible with a monistic view of an omnipotent ruler or omnipresent ground of being.

II.

Although we have set out to deal with the nature of the Church, we had to make these few observations on the doctrine of God because in the history of the discussion of the Church the preliminary view of God has been of crucial importance in setting the stage for ecclesiology. If one applies the concepts of dualism and monism, which we have chosen for want of a more expressive terminology, it is clear that a monistic theology allows for a doctrine of the Church either as an institution which participates in the serene sovereignty of God or as an extension of divine being pervading and perfecting the chaos of potential being in the world. A dualistic theology in the historical, non-ontological sense, indicated above, would lead rather to a view of the Church as the gathered community trekking through history while drawn into God's struggle for survival and upheld by the first gifts of the Spirit—a Church indefectible and infallible, not because of participation in divine being, but because of God's gift of perseverance and obedience.

Traditional Roman Catholic ecclesiology has shown a clear preference for the implications of a monistic theology. It has interpreted the Church as the Mystical Body of Christ and described it as a perfect society. There has always been a deep awareness here of the reality of the power of evil, but it was located outside the Church. Not because of historical intervention on the part of God but because of a lasting divine endowment to the Church, the institution of the Church could be regarded as free from the stain of sin, indefectible and infallible. By distinguishing between the institution of the Church and the community of the faithful, it could be admitted that there are individual sinners in the Church. But the Church itself was regarded as "holy" in the sense of "sinless." From patristic times onward the channel of communication with the original divine endowment was described in terms of Apostolic Succession. In the course of nineteen centuries the experience of the deep inroads of sin and untruth within the ranks of the Church led to an increasingly stricter and restricted view of the mode of this Apostolic Succession, so that via the emphasis on episcopal succession the idea of a basically papal succession could be formulated in 1870.

The point of departure for the ecclesiology of the Reformers was the painful experience that episcopal succession proved to be no guarantee of truth. Only gradually were the implications of this experience grasped by the Reformers.

John Calvin's famous letter to Cardinal Sadolet remains one of the most explicit documents bearing on this very point. Referring to the first-generation reformers, Calvin writes in 1539: "One thing in particular made me averse to those new teachers, namely reverence for the Church. But, when once I opened my ears and allowed myself to be taught, I saw that this fear of derogating from the majesty of the Church was groundless. For they reminded me how great the difference is between schism from the Church and studying to correct the faults by which the Church herself is contaminated." [2] The basic dilemma for such an ecumenically oriented man as Calvin comes through in an earlier passage in this same letter: ". . . if I desired to be at peace with those who boasted of being the heads of the Church and the pillars of faith, I had to purchase it with the denial of truth." [3]

With the young Luther we note from the very beginning his rootage in the medieval tradition which emphasizes the succession of the Doctors as a necessary complement to the succession of the Bishops. Yet it is with great hesitancy and tardiness that he comes to realize that the majority of the bishops close their ears to his doctoral witness and that he has to reconceive his doctrine of the Church.

In either case, with both Luther and Calvin there is a deep awareness that the Church is no holy realm, no evil-proof exten-

[2] John Calvin, *Theological Treatises*, edited by J. K. S. Reid ("Library of Christian Classics," Vol. XXII; Philadelphia, 1954), p. 252.
[3] *Ibid.*, p. 249.

sion of God's sovereignty or being, but that at times the Church may seem to be a better instrument for the devil than for God. Luther's later references to the pope as the Anti-Christ are well known. But Calvin could also say: "Nor did I think that I dissented from thy Church, because I was at war with those leaders [the bishops]. For thou didst forewarn us both by thy Son and by the Apostles that into that place would rise persons to whom I ought by no means to consent. Christ predicted not of strangers, but of men who would pass themselves off as pastors, that they would be ravenous wolves and false prophets. . . ." [4]

In our time important changes have taken place within Roman Catholic ecclesiology: the emphasis has shifted from the image of a perfect society to that of the pilgrimaging people of God and the office of the bishop is being recovered by extending the papal succession again to the succession of truth through the whole college of bishops. A *rapprochement* within the Western tradition may seem a real possibility in view of the fact that also within the Protestant communities the importance of the bishop's office is receiving new attention.

Two factors implied in the foregoing should, however, be taken into consideration. In the first place, whatever the chances are for the development of a Protestant doctrine of the bishop—drawing upon significant episcopal trends in sixteenth-century Reformation theology and upon the expanding episcopal tradition within the World Council of Churches—there is the historical experience and vivid recollection that (whatever the extent of contemporary Roman Catholic renewal may be), in the sixteenth century and in centuries before and after, institutional continuity proved to be no guarantee for the preservation of truth. Growth in Protestant ecclesiology can be noted and expected in a greater emphasis on the visibility of the Church and a de-individualization of the gifts of perseverance and obedience. But whereas Protestantism is thus in the process of repossessing its own Catholic heritage, it is unrealistic to expect that it will ever be able to regard episcopal succession as a guarantee of truth.

Alongside this crucial factor for the Reformation tradition there

[4] *Ibid.*

75

is in the second place a seeming ecumenical consensus on the doctrine of the Church. But, although historical terminology, such as the "people of God," has been introduced in the Constitution on the Church, the fundamental monistic view of God is by no means eradicated. Because the characteristics of God's being are transferred to the Church, the historical promises are changed into supernatural attributes. The tradition of submission through obedience of will and mind and the emergence of the Church as *regula proxima veritatis,* as a more immediate standard of truth than Scripture, are indicative of the fact that such promises as indefectibility and infallibility are not understood as applying to the eschatological remnant community but rather to the hierarchy and most particularly to the papal succession.

III.

The above does not provide a diversified or detailed analysis of contemporary trends in Western theology. It does indicate, however, the differences in presupposition which deeply affect the Rome-Reformation discussion about the nature of the Church. The participation of two new partners in this dialogue prevents it from stalling in a deadlocked and sterile reiteration of traditional positions. The Western dialogue can be enriched by a new exposure to aspects of the Jewish-biblical and Eastern traditions which provide a new context of discussion.

The Western innovation in the Creed, the *Nicaenoconstantinopolitanum,* usually referred to as the *filioque,* entailed the procession or mission of the Spirit from the Father *and from the Son.* This change is, of course, significant for the relation of pneumatology and Christology. For the doctrine of the Church, the *filioque* is important in those traditions where the Church is regarded as the continuation of the Incarnation. The Church, seen as the continuing life of Christ, is thus the basis of operation of the Spirit and possesses the Spirit, is coextensive with the Spirit. The extent of the shift implied in the addition of the *filioque* can be well illustrated with reference to a passage in Irenaeus's *Adver-*

sus haereses. In Book III, Chapter XXIV, 1, we read: "Ubi enim ecclesia, ibi et Spiritus Dei et ubi Spiritus Dei, ibi ecclesia et omnis gratia," where the Church is, there is the Spirit *and* where the Spirit is, there is the Church and all grace. In the Western Roman Catholic tradition the *filioque* is further unfolded in an *ecclesiaque* by isolating the first part of this sentence: "Where the Church is, there is the Spirit." The mediaeval spiritualistic sects and the Radical Reformation have isolated the second part by one-sidedly contending that "where the Spirit is, there is the Church," thus threatening the institutional aspects of the Church.

The truly Catholic view of the Church, more or less explicit in the theology of the Catholic Reformers—Luther, Zwingli, and Calvin—presupposes this interdependence of the two parts of Irenaeus's statement, counteracting the thrust from the *filioque* to the *ecclesiaque*. The relation between Church and Spirit is a relation of faith and confession; for that very reason we do not believe *in* the Church (*credere in ecclesiam*) as we believe in God (*credere in Deum*), but we believe or hold one catholic Church (*credere ecclesiam*), the communion of saints, upheld and guided by God the Spirit in all truth.

Here again we encounter the issue we raised at the beginning. Monistic theology opts for the *ecclesiaque* and—as we indicated—designates continuity and truth as qualities of the Church's being. Dualistic theology is ready to emphasize that the Church is to be *led* into truth and to be *upheld* by the Spirit. A fine specimen of this theology can be found in the Helsinki draft "Rechtfertigung heute" reworked in the 1964 Pullach proposal of the theological committee of the Lutheran World Council: "The Christian lives not for his own glory. When he accepts God's justifying judgment, this can only take place in continuous penance. Through this judgment the Church receives the courage to live amidst its enemies. Justification protects the Church against the danger of always wanting to be in the right." [5]

Whereas an exposure to the Eastern tradition may prove to be a stimulant to reconsider the implications of the addition of the

[5] *Rechtfertigung heute: Studien und Berichte* (Stuttgart, 1965), S. 17; ET *Justification Today* (Supplement to *Lutheran World*, XII [1965]), p. 8.

filioque, significant advances in biblical studies have an even more immediate bearing on our understanding of the nature of the Church. Professor Krister Stendahl of Harvard University is currently developing a thesis whose essential points he has already been able to document. Staying close to his own choice of words, we can set out the issue most sharply by saying that the problem for "modern"—as one could argue "post-Chalcedonian" (451) —theology is the Second Coming of Christ, about which the Church and its theologians speak hesitantly or are completely silent, leaving this area of the Last Things preferably to the sects. The relatively certain and clear point of departure seems to be the first coming of Christ and his earthly ministers. In extensive layers of the New Testament witness, the order of certainty and problematics is exactly the reverse. There the Second Coming of the Christ and of his Kingdom is the point of departure, the center of worship and teaching. The difficulty here is how to relate the One who comes to the earthly ministry of Jesus. A revealing example is the Matthean version of the Lord's Prayer (6:9–15). "To Matthew the Lord's Prayer is a prayer for the coming Kingdom. In the light of the Qumran material, it becomes more plausible that this applies to the *whole* of the prayer, not only to its first three petitions." [6] The first three petitions mean that "God is asked to let that time come when he will be the Holy One in the eyes of the nations, i.e., the coming of the Kingdom when his will is made manifest on earth." [7] This applies to the sanctification of the "Name," the prayer for the coming of the Kingdom and the manifestation of the Will of God. "Thus the ethical note is—to say the least—not at the fore in this part of the prayer. It asks for the establishment of the Kingdom of God, by God for us, not by us for God." [8] As far as the prayer for the so-called "daily bread" is concerned, "the clear reference in 1QSA ['adjuncts to the Rule'] [9]

[6] Krister Stendahl, "Prayer and Forgiveness," *Svensk Exegetisk Arsbok,* XXII–XXIII (1957–58), 75–86; 80 sqq.

[7] Krister Stendahl, "Matthew," in *Peake's Commentary on the Bible,* edited by Matthew Black and H. H. Rowley (London and New York, 1962), 680g.

[8] *Ibid.*

[9] See further Frank Moore Cross, Jr., *The Ancient Library of Qumran and Modern Biblical Studies* (rev. ed.; Garden City, N. Y., 1961), pp. 85 sqq.,

to the meals at Qumran as anticipations of the Messianic banquet, as well as the futuristic note in all forms of the words of institution to the Eucharist suggest that 'our daily bread' is the bread which is about to be given, just as the Kingdom is about to come." [10] An adoptionistic Christology—be it adoptionism at the birth, baptism, or death of Jesus—may well have been the interpretation of Jesus' ministry most congenial to the eschatological, future-oriented Galilean Christian community. For our purposes it is important to note that whereas the Logos Christology, and in the fifth century the Chalcedonian Definition, was widely accepted as the appropriate interpretation of Jesus of Nazareth in relation to the Christ, the application of two-nature Christology to the Church is a later monistic speculation which tends to obscure the pneumatological basis of the Church.

IV.

A last comment on biblical theology. The most common reference for all those who want to regard the Church as the continuation of the Incarnation is St. Paul's use of the "Body of Christ" as an image for the Church. Again a nonhistorical ontological monism has made this image a basis for far-reaching dogmatic conclusions. An analysis of all references to the Body of Christ reveals, however, that the expression is nowhere employed in an ontological sense, but rather as an image suggesting the unity of the Church, in a number of different ways. The image, "Body of Christ," should, therefore, not be used to show that according to Holy Scripture the Church is the extension of Christ in time and space, sharing therefore in Christ's attributes of divinity and infallibility. The line running through the various uses of the image in the Pauline letters is rather that none of the members is closer to the head than another, that none is the head, and that all members have only one standard: *agape*. It is on the basis of the *agape* as

pp. 234 sqq.; "The meal must be understood as a liturgical anticipation of the Messianic banquet" (p. 234).

[10] Stendahl, "Prayer and Forgiveness," p. 82.

gift of the Spirit and of its application in mutual forgiveness that the Church is given the assurance that, asking, it will be given; seeking, it will find; knocking, the doors will be opened. Thinking about indefectibility and infallibility in these terms of promises and confidence, we may hope to overcome the confessional obstacles erected by a monistic theology and radically historicize the Church as the community of memory and hope, the People of God drawn into God's fight for survival in a diabolically rebellious world, propelled towards its goal by the power of the same Spirit which anointed Jesus as the Christ, and trekking towards the Kingdom to come.

Many other aspects of the Church will be discussed or touched upon in my following papers, since one cannot speak about Scripture, Tradition, Sacrament, or grace without placing these within the context of the Body of Christ, the People of God, the *communio sanctorum*. But at this point one final observation is in order: the emphasis on the recovery of what we have called a theological dualism implies a much closer association between the people of the Old and the New Covenant. Both are confronted with the power of evil and disobedience; both proleptically participate in the messianic meal; both are strengthened by the vision of a new heaven *and* a new earth. And both are upheld and guided by the God who does not abandon the works of his hands, but remains faithful to his Covenant promises.

Scripture

I.

In the next paper on Tradition and traditions we shall direct ourselves to the problem of Scripture and Tradition. Here we want to pursue three fundamental problems which, being intimately related to the question of Scripture and Tradition, merit our special attention: the relation of the Old Testament and the New Testament, biblical hermeneutics, and the offices of Bishop and Doctor as interpreters of Scripture.

In the first paper we discussed the importance of a historical, non-ontological view of the Church as the Spirit-gathered and Spirit-driven community certain of survival and ultimate victory as the Body of Christ pilgrimaging towards the Kingdom.

At the same time Jesus' message in its most original form stressed, by contrast, the crescendo coming of the Kingdom, breaking into time, being now "among us," coming towards us rather than our trekking to him. This is another perspective of the relation of God and history, the theological parallel to the Copernican revolution. The image of the trekking people of God "en route," *in via* towards the Kingdom, clearly has advantages in stressing both the remnant character of the Church and the incompleteness of its mission. There is a less attractive side to this imagery: it suggests that the Church is moving towards the Kingdom instead of the Kingdom approaching, "coming nigh," breaking in, "among us" in several forms of which the Church is one. I regard this theology of motion and time as the Copernican revolution sparked by the Reformation, although I grant that the spiritual energies thus released have yet to be fully harnessed.

Just as Nicholas Copernicus († 1543) changed our world-view from geocentricity to heliocentricity, so his contemporaries, Luther, Zwingli, and Calvin, designated the Kingdom of God rather than the Church as the life-bringing center of the universe. This was indeed a revolution, in hindsight vis-à-vis the Eastern tradition, not insofar as the East had been willing to refer to Christ as *autobasileia* (the very Kingdom of God) but insofar as Christ became the prototype of the Church and the divinization of the faithful. Consciously and more immediately this Copernican revolution meant a break with the mediaeval Western tradition. Although St. Augustine in his *City of God* did not completely identify Church and Kingdom, the time of the Church and the millennium, the thousand years' kingdom, had in his view become coextensive.

In regard to individual Christians, it was not unusual in Western mediaeval theology to speak of the "visitation" by God, but the chief concept was that of the *viator*, the sojourner en route to God's Kingdom. This image could be applied to the whole Church as the *ecclesia militans,* militant Church as crusading army. The Copernican revolution of the Reformation, then, meant both the discovery of the *diastasis* or interval between Kingdom and Church *and* the awareness that this gap was being closed by the approach of the Kingdom. This proved to have immense implications for ecclesiology and the doctrine of Justification. As we shall indicate in the paper on grace, God's approach to man (his justification of the sinner on the level of the sinner) is one of the chief characteristics of Reformation insight into the mystery of the *iustificatio impii.* In regard to ecclesiology it meant, at one and the same time, a reduction of the mediaeval doctrine of the two swords to the older doctrine of the two keys and a recovery of the role of the State in the coming of the Kingdom. The temporal claims of the mediaeval Church and its aspirations to play *a* or *the* political role—continued within the Roman Catholic Church in the papal state and present-day Vatican City—gave way in the Reformation tradition to a new understanding of the duality of State and Church as signs of the Kingdom.[1]

We are here concerned with the implications of this Copernican revolution for an understanding of the relation of the Old Testament and the New Testament, for biblical hermeneutics and the relative roles of Bishop and Doctor.

With a lopsided emphasis on the Church as community of *viatores,* it is almost impossible to retain the Old Testament as a charter of God's rule over his people for the purpose of communion with them. In terms of a progressive development from the fallen state of mankind, to the election of Israel, to the Old Covenant, to the New Covenant in Christ stretching out towards the Kingdom, the Old Testament appears to be a primitive stage dated and abrogated by the coming of Christ. The dangers of such an escalation-view of history are particulary evident in our time. Now, in all sectors of Christianity, we are in the process of becoming a New Testament Christianity. Marcion, who rejected the Old Testament as the revelation of an alien God, has proved to be one of the most successful heretics of all time. I regard it as a great

[1] Cf. my article, "Protestant Reflections on Church and State," *Theology and Life,* IV (1961), 60 sqq.

threat that theology has now been largely reduced to soteriology, community with God spiritualized into communion with God, liturgy (service) confined to (Sunday) worship, and creation understood as the context rather than the goal of redemption. Due to this complex of reductions, often referred to in the United States as "pietism," Christianity seems redundant if not an obstacle to the construction of "the Great Society" and the Church of Christ irrelevant compared to the Peace Corps. A New Testament Christianity which has virtually abrogated the Old Testament can place Jesus Christ in a context of its own choosing: it does not make any difference whether this context is gnostic eternal truth, the inner life of the Spirit, mystical ascent, or the kingdom of the Church.

In a precious booklet entitled *Die Christliche Kirche und das Alte Testament*, Arnold A. van Ruler formulates this by saying: "The Old Testament is necessary for the Christian Church, because it gives the legitimate interpretation of the Gospel. Without it Christ and his Kingdom, intended also for the Gentiles, cannot be completely understood. Unless the Gentiles continuously interpret the Gospel from the point of view of the Old Testament, they are necessarily making something else out of it, introducing alien concepts and sometimes changing these into their opposite." [2] Van Ruler goes on to say that this is the case in a historical sense: the Old Testament is the historical background for the New Testament. But this has also theological implications; the Gentiles lose sight of the royal office of Christ: "They limit themselves to the sacerdotal office; or to his Person, through which comes the forgiving love of God; or to his ethical teaching and his moral example; or to the great mystic, the leader in the mystical choir of humanity. But they overlook or as often spiritualize [and thus suppress] the fact that he is king, the *kurios*, and more specifically the King of Kings and the Lord of Lords over the earth, reaching deeply into the political dimension. The Kingdom of Jesus comes through—and as the heart of the matter—when the Gospel is seen in the light of the Old Testament. Then the Gospel proves to be a thoroughly historical reality and thoroughly profane and earthy." [3]

[2] Munich, 1955; S. 74.
[3] *Ibid.*, S. 75.

83

Although the recovery of the Old Testament is a formidable ecumenical task, it should be pointed out that the relation of the Old and New Testaments, as I see it, bears directly not only upon the quest of our generation for the relevance of the Christian Gospel in a secularized world but also upon the relation of Christianity and Judaism. The unfortunate history of the Vatican II discussion of a draft on the relation of the Roman Catholic Church and the Jews has given credence to the view that the crux of the matter is the establishment of the guilt of the Jews and of the willingness of the Roman Catholic Church to extend forgiveness to the Jews. Due to the nexus between the Roman Catholic Church and the Vatican State, this has by now become a political issue vis-à-vis the Arab nations; and, due to centuries of pogroms, Jewish communities have been brought to the point where they openly and repeatedly have stated their appreciation of such a declaration.

However important it admittedly is to eradicate the stubborn roots of anti-Semitism, the Christian dialogue with Judaism, springing from wartime experiences, looks beyond religious liberty and political-social equality to a theological *resourcement*, a return to the sources. Just as we have to draw on the Old Testament as the vital context for true understanding of the Gospel, so the Church of the Gentiles is grafted onto the original tree of Israel, and our Christian hope for the establishment of a new heaven and a new earth is intimately interwoven with the fate and future of the Chosen People of Israel.

Severing their ties with the Old Testament heritage through allegory and countless apologies *contra Judaeos*, early Church Fathers could claim the title "New Israel" and imply with that the abrogation of the former Covenant promises to the people of Israel. The tendency in the West to contrast the Old Testament as *timor* (fear) with the New Testament as *amor* (love) has had disastrous consequences both for the theology of the Church and the action of the Christian State in the Middle Ages. The Lutheran dialectic between Law and Gospel can indeed only be understood within this mediaeval setting. It is misunderstood when identified with the mediaeval contrast between *timor* and *amor*.

The Copernican revolution of the Reformation in the distinction and reversal of Church and Kingdom allows and calls for an appreciation of the full canonicity of the Old Testament, the importance of its earthy realism, and its necessary role as demythologizer of pagan interpretations of the New Testament witness.

II.

In turning to biblical hermeneutics, we limit the scope of our discussion to the relation of the literal and the spiritual senses of Scripture. As history shows, this is intimately related to the reception of the Old Testament by the Christian Church.

Since the early days of the Christian Church, the Old Testament has posed the chief exegetical problem to biblical interpreters. The New Testament has seemed clear and straightforward by comparison. The Gospels contain the history of Jesus Christ while the other writings contain principally the interpretation of this history and its application to the life of the Church. But how can one apply the Old Testament to Christ? How can one make good the claim of the Church that the Books of Moses are her books? The Apostolic writings are themselves a constant reminder of the place and function of the Old Testament at the very beginnings of the Church before the formation of the New Testament canon, when "the Scriptures" meant only one thing, namely, what later came to be looked upon as the Old Testament.

Jesus, Peter, and Paul had appealed to "the Scriptures" as prophecy of the events now fulfilled or in the process of being fulfilled. The Apologetes, such as Justin Martyr († *ca.* 165), used the Old Testament to prove that Christianity was not an innovation but older than any of the other respected traditions. In his famous Dialogue with Trypho, a Jewish teacher, Justin argued that every move and word of Christ had been predicted in the Old Testament. At the other end of the spectrum the Gnostics or gnosticizing Christians, embarrassed by the anthropomorphic descriptions of the Old Testament God—as one who gets angry, laughs and changes his mind—were intent on showing behind the outer crust of the mere letter of the text the hidden meaning discernible only by those with true *gnosis* (knowledge, understanding). Their apologetic stance against Hellenistic philosophies required an immutable and immovable God rather than the "movable" God of the Jewish Scriptures.

The most radical position of all was taken by Marcion († *ca.* 160), the founder of a large church which was not absorbed into Manicheism until the end of the third century. In his *Antithesis* he rejected the Old Testament completely: the God of the Old Testament is for him an absolute antithesis to the God of the New Testament. The God of the Law has nothing to do with the God of Jesus Christ, the God of Love. Hence he rejected the allegorical [4] method of interpreting the Old Testament, which had served the apologetic enterprise of the Church so well against both Jewish and philosophical traditions.

Although Marcion's concern is indicative of digestive disorders in the very system of the Church occasioned by its efforts to absorb Jewish tradition, his solution was not determinative for the future. In the rabbinic exegesis of "the Scriptures" and in the Greek philosophical interpretation of Homer, the allegorical method had been employed; furthermore, St. Paul had used the term in Galatians 4:24: "These things contain an allegory." In the Alexandrian school of Clement († *ca.* 215) and Origen († 254) this method was further developed, probably under the influence of Philo († 50).[5] For Philo, as for Clement and Origen, the use of allegory to search for the meaning hidden in the text did not imply the rejection of the letter. Actually, Origen admitted a literal, moral,

[4] Here we use the term in its general sense of nonliteral interpretation. In a more precise usage, it came to stand for one of three spiritual senses together with the tropological (moral) and anagogical (eschatological) senses. See further below.

[5] See the important chapter, "The Allegorical Method," in Harry Austryn Wolfson, *The Philosophy of the Church Fathers*, Vol. I: *Faith, Trinity, Incarnation* (2d ed.; Cambridge, Mass., 1964), pp. 24–72; further bibliography there. Cf. Robert M. Grant, *The Letter and the Spirit* (London, 1957), pp. 121 sqq.

and spiritual sense in correspondence with his understanding of man as body, soul, and spirit. Insofar, however, as the spirit is infinitely higher than the body, the allegorical sense is clearly superior to the letter in which it is contained. The school of Antioch, on the other hand, while not rejecting the allegorical method, used it sparingly. Yet its most articulate representative, St. John Chrysostom, rejected it out of hand. The discussion of the relation of letter and spirit, of word and intention, became a significant factor in the Christological debates which dealt with the relation of the human and the divine nature of Christ. The question whether one finds the *spirit* through the letter (Alexandria's emphasis on the spiritual sense) or rather finds the Spirit through the *letter* (Antioch's emphasis on the literal sense) is clearly related to the Christological debates of the fourth and fifth centuries. Antioch, interested in the historical reality of Jesus, the Christ, would emphasize that God was in *Christ*. Alexandria, concerned with preserving the unity between God, the creator and ruler of the cosmos, and the Incarnate God, stressed rather that *God* was in Christ.

For a time the problem of the Old Testament did not seem acute and the exegetical issue was subordinated to the Christological problem. In 451, at the Fourth Ecumenical Council of Chalcedon, the Christological extremes on both sides were condemned; it was not until 553, at the Fifth Ecumenical Council of Constantinople, that the two exegetical extremes, Origenistic speculation and Antiochian literalism, were stamped as heretical.

St. Augustine, the founding father of the Western exegetical tradition, in his conversion to Christianity, experienced the exegetical problem as central. In his *Confessions*, Book VI, Chapters III–V, he describes how much he owed in this respect to his bishop, Ambrose of Milan. For a considerable period Augustine had been attracted by Manicheism, which had been keen to show—with the same literal approach as Marcion's—how the use of the Old Testament necessarily led to absurdities. The sermons of Ambrose clarified for Augustine how, through the use of allegory, the Old Testament yielded its innermost secrets. This did not imply a disregard for the letter: to ward off uncontrollable

87

allegorical speculation he stated that "it is most shameful to interpret a particular text allegorically if not clearly supported elsewhere by non-allegorical, literal interpretation." Thus the concerns of Origen and Chrysostom had been reconciled; the schools of Alexandria and Antioch had found a common heir. This aspect of St. Augustine's thought would provide a basis for later developments.[6]

Yet Augustine's rules for the exegesis of Holy Scripture were part of his total view of the nature of theology which would not satisfy the scientific requirements of twelfth-century and thirteenth-century theologians. For him there is no objective standard by which to separate the literal sense—or the clear places in Scripture—from the allegorical sense—or the obscure places. The difference is not in the text and therefore is not scientifically (uncommittedly!) discernible, but largely depends on the relation of the reader to God. In his chief hermeneutical work, "On Christian Doctrine," he says that the way to differentiate between the two senses is to find out whether the text elicits one's love and faith; if so, it is to be taken literally; if not, it is apparently allegory: "Whatever there is in the Word of God that cannot, when taken literally, be referred either to purity of life or soundness of doctrine is to be classified as figurative."[7] If constant meditation is required to yield love for God and neighbor, a text is obscure and allegorical; if not, the text can be taken literally.[8] The allegorical sense differs, therefore, from the literal sense insofar as it is not immediately accessible or "fruitful." Not the meaning but the mode of understanding is different.

Allegory has the great advantage of humiliating human pride; it

---

[6] See Beryl Smalley, *The Study of the Bible in the Middle Ages* (2d ed.; Oxford, 1952). In French: C. Spicq, *Esquisse d'une histoire de l'exégèse latine au Moyen Age* (Paris, 1944), and Henri de Lubac, S.J., *Exégèse médiévale: Les quatre sens de l'Ecriture* (2 vols., each with two parts; Paris, 1959–64), especially Volume II, Part II. In German: Gerhard Ebeling, *Evangelische Evangelienauslegung* (2. Aufl.; Darmstadt, 1962); "Die Anfänge von Luthers Hermeneutik," *Zeitschrift für Theologie und Kirche,* XLVIII (1951), 172–230; "Hermeneutik," in *Die Religion in Geschichte und Gegenwart,* Bd. III (Tübingen, 1959), Sp. 242–62 (further bibliography there, Sp. 258–62).

[7] *De doctrina Christiana,* III, x, 14.

[8] *Ibid.,* xv, 23.

exercises the mind in true piety; and above all it separates the readers into two groups, the truly pious who persevere in their ardent search and the unworthy and indifferent investigators.[9] Languages, history, biology, astronomy, and dialectics are great tools: "But when the student of Scripture, thus prepared, starts his investigation, let him constantly meditate upon the saying of the Apostle, 'knowledge puffs up, but love builds up' (1 Cor. 8:1). For so he will feel that whatever may be the riches he brings with him out of Egypt, yet unless he has kept the Passover, he cannot be safe. . . . Only when he is meek and humble, carrying the easy yoke of Christ and laden with his light burden, does the knowledge of the Scripture not puff him up." [10]

In a bold effort to summarize St. Augustine's hermeneutics in one sentence one can say: God the author of Scripture speaks through Scripture to two kinds of audience in two modes with the one purpose of fostering faith and love.

When, due to the scientific revolution of the twelfth century, Scripture became the *object* of study rather than the *subject* through which God speaks to the student, the difference between the two modes of speaking was investigated in terms of the texts themselves rather than in their relation to the recipients. The literal sense of Scripture was increasingly analyzed as one would study any other literary document. St. Thomas Aquinas is the culmination of a development fostered by Hugh and Andrew of St. Victor (early twelfth century) which would pay increasing attention to the literal sense of Holy Scripture and seek to find objective standards to define its nature. Here we stand at the cradle of our modern standards for "sound" biblical exegesis. Andrew had little hesitance in availing himself of "the riches of Egypt." He, as Thomas Aquinas and Nicolas of Lyra († 1349), liberally drew on the resources of contemporary Jewish exegetes.[11] Yet it remained to

[9] Jean Pépin shows that Augustine in this high evaluation of allegory draws upon Clement and Origen as well as upon Graeco-Roman pagan theology: "Saint Augustin et la fonction protreptique de l'allégorie," *Recherches augustiniennes*, I (1958), 243–86.

[10] *De doctrina Christiana*, II, xli, 62; xlii, 63.

[11] See, for example, the excellent study by Herman Hailperin, *Rashi and the Christian Scholars* (Pittsburgh, 1963).

be determined how "the riches of Egypt" related to "the riches of the New Israel" and whose competence it was to relate these two realms.

We have been relatively detailed in our notes on the Augustinian position and its prehistory because the Augustinian position is in our time better known as fundamentalism, still a vital force in the Roman Catholic and Protestant Western Churches. The scientific revolution of the twelfth century has its close parallel in the upheaval wrought by biblical criticism in the late eighteenth and nineteenth centuries. The late mediaeval efforts to preserve the accomplishments of this revolution and its anti-revolutionary reactions are worth noting, both as context for the Reformation and as parallels to our own situation.

Thomas's distinction between the spiritual and literal senses of Scripture, shifted by Lyra and his followers to the double literal sense of Scripture, allowed for a combination of *sapientia* and *scientia*, theological meditation upon the meaning intended by the divine author *and* scholarly analysis of the intention of the historical author.

In the Introduction to his *Quincuplex Psalterium* (Paris, 1509) Faber Stapulensis rejected this distinction and contended that the spiritual sense *is* the literal sense, and vice versa. At the same time it is clear that for him the spiritual (i.e., the literal) sense is not attainable through simple grammatical exegesis. The unbeliever cannot discover the real meaning because he approaches the text without the most necessary exegetical tool of all, namely, that self-same Spirit which created Scripture. A century earlier another Frenchman, Jean Gerson, had also claimed that mere grammatical analysis will not yield the true literal sense. Nevertheless, Gerson fought quite a different battle which led him in a very different, even radically opposite, direction.

Faber deplores the influence of "rabbinic" exegesis upon the Christian interpretation of the Scriptures, for he feels that the uninspired "rabbinic" reading of Scripture reveals nothing more than "the letter which kills," the naked letter, *sola littera*. To discover the true meaning of Scripture, its true literal sense, he turns to "our first leaders, the Apostles, the Evangelists, and the

Prophets." Though he grants that he is not a prophet himself, he draws upon these men who saw God with their own eyes and heard him speak with their own ears. Thus he is helped to discern the true literal sense, for the most part "by the joint witness of the Scriptures."

Gerson, on the other hand, directs his defense of the true literal sense against the Hussites, who—as he reports—have been able to find supporters in England, Scotland, Prague, Germany, and "yes, O horror, even in France . . . They disseminate heresies and oppose the truth which they acknowledge or should acknowledge, since they call themselves Catholics: they say that their doctrines are based on Scripture and Scripture's literal sense which they call 'Scripture alone.' " [12]

Gerson does not oppose *sola littera*, as does Faber, but *sola Scriptura*, not the isolated and naked letter, but the isolated and naked Scripture. With Faber he turns to "the first leaders" to discover the true literal sense, but he does not find it by means of "the joint witness of Scripture" but by means of the tradition of the Church: "The literal sense of Scripture was first revealed by Christ and the Apostles, illustrated by miracles, confirmed by the blood of martyrs; the holy Doctors further developed the truths implied in this literal sense by their alert and learned warfare against the heretics; finally these truths were officially defined by the Holy Councils." [13] In short, "the literal sense of Scripture is not to be defined in terms of the insights of any given individual but in terms of the decisions of the Church, inspired and governed by the Holy Spirit." [14]

It is noteworthy that Luther in his first commentary on Scripture, on the Psalms (1513–1516), takes up the battle cries of both Gerson and Faber by opposing at once "the arbitrary exegesis of

[12] "Quam solam scripturam dicunt. . . . De sensu litterali sacrae scripturae et de causis errantium," in *Opera omnia*, edited by L. E. Du Pin (5 vols.; Antwerp, 1706), Vol. I, col. 2 A.

[13] *Ibid.*, col. 3 C.

[14] *Ibid.*, col. 3 A. When Gerson argues in another treatise that the literal sense is to be drawn from "Scripture in its context" (*ex circumstantiis scripturae*) the Church is to be regarded as the most crucial part of this context. Cf. "Declaratio compendiosa quae veritates sint credendae de necessitate salutis," in *Opera omnia*, Vol. I, col. 24 B.

the heretics" and the threat of "the letter which kills." In his exposition of Psalm 1:2, "in His law does he [the righteous] meditate day and night," Luther points to the Judaizers who continue to kill the prophets of God, as the Jews of the Old Covenant had before, "by smothering the Word of God, that is, its living sense intended by the Holy Spirit." Secondly, there are those who meditate on the law, but not on the law of God; the canon lawyers, the arbitrary exegetes, meditate on human laws and human traditions such as the decretals of the popes. Ultimately, however, these Judaizers and heretics all fall into one and the same category: their meditation is not in "the law, but the law is in them," and thus they prove their own opinions by the authority of Scripture.[15] Luther pursues in this early stage the battle of both Gerson and Faber, without, however, admitting of a two-front war. In his later works the two fronts come to coincide completely and to delineate the common basis for his doctrine of the authority of Scripture and his doctrine of justification in which a sharp contrast is drawn between the Gospel and the law.

For the purpose of this paper it will be enough to indicate that another line parallel to the one from Lyra through Burgos, Perez, Faber to Luther can be traced running via Gerson in the direction of the Counter Reformation. The Introduction to Prierias's *Aurea Rosa* of 1503 is an elaborate hermeneutical treatise, "The Rules for the Exegesis of Holy Scripture." Here the identification of literal and spiritual senses which we met with Faber is rejected as untenable. In line with—and actually quoting—Thomas, Lyra, and Burgos, Prierias argues that there is one literal sense which is subject to human investigation, and another literal sense—and here a Gersonian emphasis comes through—which is derived from the teaching authority of the Church. In case the Doctors of the Church should not agree in their exegesis, there is not merely a twofold but a manifold literal sense in Scripture, although it never concerns truths necessary for salvation and authoritatively taught by the Church.

In his first attack on Luther in 1518 Prierias spells out what such

[15] Weimarer Ausgabe (henceforth, WA), 55.II.1.13,14–14,22. This section dates from Autumn, 1516.

a view of Scripture implies for the relationship between Scripture and Tradition: "Whoever does not rely on the teaching of the Roman Church and the Roman Pontiff as the infallible rule of faith, from which also Holy Scripture draws its power and authority, is a heretic." [16]

During the sixteenth-century confessional debates, the problem of the relation between Scripture and tradition of the Church assumed a place of pre-eminence. The first stirrings of biblical criticism in the eighteenth century increasingly refocused the attention of biblical scholars on the question of the interdependence of the literal and spiritual senses of the Bible. Whatever the emphases may have been in different periods of history, the intimate bond between these two issues is undeniable and actually plays an important part in the ecumenical dialogue in the mid-twentieth century. The discussion of the so-called *sensus plenior* [17] and the distinction between *Historie* and *Geschichte*,[18] so central in the work of Rudolf Bultmann, are sufficient proof of the on-going concern with the problem of exegesis of Holy Scripture.

For contemporary discussion, three points seem of overriding importance:

1. The solution of Prierias implies the absorption of the office of the Doctor of Scripture by the office of the Bishop, i.e., the Pope. As we hope to show in our next paper this absorption has actually taken place in the Roman communion.

2. The recovery of the full canonicity of the Old Testament gives the context of interpretation of the New Testament which makes it possible for Scripture to speak to the Church: *scriptura suiipsius interpres.*

3. If the two-source theory of Trent is going to be replaced, do not allow new twins to take its place. The disjunction of Word

[16] "In praesumptuosas Martini Lutheri conclusiones de potestate papae dialogus," Fundamentum tertium, in Valentin Ernst Löschern, *Vollständige Reformations—Acta und Documenta*, Bd. II (Leipzig, 1722), S. 15.

[17] "The sensus plenior is that additional, deeper meaning intended by God, but not clearly intended by the human author . . ." (R. E. Brown, *The Sensus Plenior of Sacred Scripture* [Baltimore, 1955], p. 92).

[18] Here *Historie* stands for the collection of external data and *Geschichte* is the existential interpretation of the meaning of historical events.

and Spirit, opposed by Faber and Luther, is again advocated in our day by the most attractive school in contemporary Roman Catholic theology. Thus Yves Congar can say, "Notons que l'enseignement salutaire ou évangelique nous est livré sous deux formes et selon deux modes: le document et l'éducation, le texte et l'esprit vivant." The contrast between "the text" and "the living Spirit" represents that same disastrous dualism which in the past undercut the authority of the Old Testament, and today threatens to make Scripture an extension of the Church.

TRADITION AND TRADITIONS

I.

The traditional way to discuss Scripture in the context of an interconfessional dialogue has been to pose the problem, "Scripture and Tradition." Oriented to this issue is also the enumeration of the properties of Scripture in Protestant dogmatics: *auctoritas* and *certitudo*, *sufficientia* and *perfectio*, *necessitas* and *perspicuitas*. But all these properties of Scripture have received their peculiar edge within the setting of the question, "Scripture and Tradition," or—to follow its formulation by the Fourth World Conference (Montreal,1963) on Faith and Order—"Tradition and Traditions." [1] As we saw, one cannot turn to any such issue as the relation of the Old Testament and the New Testament, biblical hermeneutics, or the relation of Bishop and Doctor without encountering at every juncture this crucial problem.

Before we deal with this issue, a few introductory remarks with regard to the *material* and *formal* sufficiency of Holy Scripture are in order. The first of these problems is concerned with the question whether all truths are contained in Holy Scripture; the second with the question whether Holy Scripture is the most immediate

---

[1] See *Report on Tradition and Traditions* (Faith and Order Paper, No. 40; Geneva, 1963). Also Yves M.-J. Congar, O.P., *La Tradition et les traditions* (2 vols.; Paris, 1960–63).

authority for life and faith. The first problem—that of the material sufficiency—has drawn most of the attention in these last decades. The second problem, however, is ultimately more decisive. The first problem touches upon the question whether there are one or more sources for Revelation—so hotly debated on the Council floor in the first session of the Second Vatican Council and in many Council reports ever since. The second issue—that of the formal sufficiency of Holy Scripture—is ultimately more important, because it touches upon the question in what way Holy Scripture can be given a platform from which it can accompany, guide, and correct the life and teachings of the Church.

II.

Now when we first turn to the issue of the material sufficiency of Holy Scripture, it should be noted that the Reformation slogan, *sola Scriptura*, has at least this meaning, that all truth is contained in Holy Scripture not merely in the rational sense that it contains a number of revealed truths, but in the sense that God speaks through Holy Scripture without omitting anything necessary for salvation. This *sola Scriptura* has often been misunderstood as implying the rejection of Tradition as such. An analysis of sixteenth-century debates shows that it actually means the rejection of a particular concept of Tradition.

In the sixteenth century, Scripture and Tradition were not mutually exclusive options, but a clash occurred between two concepts of Tradition—the exegetical tradition of interpreted Scripture, which we like to call Tradition I, and the two-sources theory which allows for an extra-biblical oral tradition, which we like to call Tradition II. Although this is still subject to discussion, it seems clear to me that the Council of Trent opted for Tradition II, whereas the Reformation tradition opted for Tradition I.

Both concepts of Tradition find their mediaeval partisans. In the early Middle Ages, Tradition I and Tradition II cannot be clearly separated for the simple reason that those who *de facto* hold Tradition II, continue to declare themselves in favor of the material sufficiency of Holy Scripture.[2] But once such Nominalists as Occam, Gerson, D'Ailly, and Biel have prepared the way for the reception of Tradition II, the historian is in a better position to discern the contrast. As long as his eyes are still blinded, however, by the conventional contrast of Scripture versus tradition, he is bound to err in his interpretation of the sources.[3]

Fourteenth-century and fifteenth-century theologians like John Wycliff, John Hus, and Wessel Gansfort do not defend Scripture against Tradition, but they pose Tradition I against Tradition II. True to Vincent of Lérins' five restrictive requirements for an authoritative tradition, they defend along with the material sufficiency of Holy Scripture the authority of the exegetical tradition whenever there is a common and explicit witness of the Fathers, in particular of the four great Western Doctors of the Church: Augustine, Jerome, Ambrose, and Gregory.

By way of summary of this position it may be said that these representatives of Tradition I do not deny the importance and validity of episcopal succession for the preservation of the truth. They indeed regard Tradition as the execution of the custodian's task in the Church. But in contrast to those holding to Tradition II, their emphasis falls on the *successio doctorum* rather than on the *successio episcoporum*.

Understandably, their attack is especially directed against the canon lawyers, the most conspicuous bearers of Tradition II. But they also sharply react against the theologians' practice of building Tradition into the "silent places" of Holy Scripture. In its strongest forms this criticism may lead to the transformation of Tradi-

[2] See my "*Quo Vadis?* Tradition from Irenaeus to *Humani Generis*," *Scottish Journal of Theology*, XVI (1963), 239. Josef Finkenzeller regards Duns Scotus as the turning point: "Die Tradition als ursprüngliche und unabhängige Quelle der christlichen Lehre ist in der Zeit, in der Skotus die Sentenzen kommentiert, unbekannt. . . . In der Betonung der apostolischen Tradition im Sinne einer über die Hl. Schrift hinausgehenden Ueberlieferung hat unter den Theologen der Hochscholastik Duns Skotus den entscheidenden Durchbruch gewagt . . ." (*Offenbarung und Theologie nach der Lehre des Johannes Duns Skotus* [Münster, 1960], S. 74–5.

[3] The most recent example is the well-documented essay by Michael Hurley, S.J., "Scriptura sola: Wycliff and His Critics," *Traditio*, XVI (1960), 275–352, who fails to understand Wycliff because he presses Wycliff under the yoke of the either-or of Scripture or Tradition. See, especially, pages 278–9.

tion I. Here perhaps we stand at the cradle of what is usually called biblicism, which via some branches of the Reformation and of seventeenth-century orthodoxy comes down to us in the form of fundamentalism.

On the other hand, Wessel's emphasis on the operation of the Holy Spirit and his clear distinction of Gospel and Law brings him closer, indeed remarkably close, to the positions of Luther, Melanchthon, and Calvin. Though the positions of these Reformers should be differentiated, their consensus appears in its contrasts with Tradition II.

III.

With these few words we have already suggested that as much as Trent represents Tradition II, the Reformers represent Tradition I. And our observation concerning the later Middle Ages can be applied to the period of the Reformation and Counter Reformation. We are here not confronted with the alternatives of Scripture and Tradition but with the clash of two radically different concepts of tradition, Tradition I and Tradition II. After a sketch of the concept of Tradition in its Lutheran and Tridentine formulation, we hope to have reached a vantage point which will allow us to make a few observations bearing on the contemporary scene.

There can be no doubt that one of the most essential aspects, even the very foundation of Luther's theology, is the *sola Scriptura* principle. We have seen that this principle as such does not necessarily imply a rejection of the so-called co-inherence of Church and Scripture. It indicates, however, that Luther's theological enterprise does not move within the context of Tradition II, but in that of Tradition I.

How Luther himself understood and applied this principle, however, is not easy to define in a few words.[4] One thing is clear: even

[4] A few of the most important secondary sources are: Otto Scheel, *Luthers Stellung zur Heiligen Schrift* (Tübingen, 1902); Paul Althaus, "Gehorsam und Freiheit in Luthers Stellung zur Bibel," *Luther*, IX (1927), 74 sqq.; Heinrich Bornkamm, *Das Wort Gottes bei Luther* (Berlin, 1933); J. M. Reu, *Luther and the Scriptures* (Columbus, Ohio, 1944); Ragnar Bring, *Luthers*

if one is not willing to distinguish between a "young Luther" and an "old Luther," one has to concede that it is misleading to rely primarily on evidence drawn from the pre-1522 period. Luther is one of the most striking examples of a "contextual" theologian. Especially in his letters and treatises, he does not write in a well-balanced, scholarly *summa* style by reasoning from principle to application. His writing is in the pastoral sense of the word "opportunistic," *situationsbedingt*, and the interpreter therefore has to take the relevant situation into serious consideration to discover the underlying principles.

One does not need therefore to fall back on a development-hypothesis to point out that in the first five years Luther's primary purpose was to contrast the teachings of Holy Scripture with papal decisions. In the first period Luther emphasizes the authority of Scripture over against "human additions." Though in 1518—at the time of his Augsburg debate with Cajetan—he is still willing to accept papal decrees as secondary sources, he has already rejected the Tradition II concept.[5] The burning of the books of canon law

Anschauung von der Bibel (Berlin, 1951); Regin Prenter, *Spiritus Creator* (Philadelphia, 1953); H. Oestergaard-Nielsen, *Scriptura sacra et viva vox: Eine Lutherstudie* (Berlin, 1957).

[5] J. N. Bakhuizen van den Brink has noted—and criticized—the fact that the editors of the *Konkordienbuch* (Göttingen, 1930) refer in the Index from "Tradition" to "Menschensatzungen": "La Tradition dans l'Eglise primitive et au XVIe siècle," *Revue d'histoire et de philosophie religieuses*, XXXVI (1956), 272-3. See the same in *The Book of Concord* (Philadelphia, 1959), *sub voce*. When one checks the references it appears that not "tradition" but "traditions" are meant which are identified with "observances": "We gladly keep the old traditions set up in the Church because they are useful and promote tranquillity, and we interpret them in an evangelical way [by] excluding the opinion that holds that they justify" (*Apology of the Augsburg Confession*, art. xv). As proved to be the case with Gabriel Biel, these traditions are understood to be rites and observances. They are rejected as the work of "summists and canonists," who neglected "more important things such as faith, consolation in severe trials, and the like" (*Augsburg Confession*, art. xxvi). These statements do not refer to what we termed Tradition I. J. T. Mueller's *Die symbolischen Bücher der evangelische-lutherischen Kirche* (Stuttgart, 1860) accurately refers to "traditiones" (S. 961). For the same use, see *The Little Catechism* of 1556 "approved by . . . John Calvin"; Answer IV in *The School of Faith*, edited by T. F. Torrance (New York, 1959), p. 239. This plural "traditiones" cannot surprise us in view of the fact that—except at two places in its *Acta*—this was the disputed term at the Council of Trent.

at the Elster Gate at Wittenberg, 10th December, 1520, is the eloquent symbol and seal of the rejection of a tradition which we found indeed to have been carried by canon lawyers.

Shortly afterwards he says: "Christ's teaching and the pope's teaching will not and cannot rule jointly, for Christ wants to be sole Master, as he says in Matthew 23:8." [6] This would be a consistent theme in Luther's theology throughout his life. But faced with the rising tide of the Radical Reformation, he expressed more clearly what the *sola Scriptura* principle positively stands for.

It is in this context that we have to search for an answer to the question as to whether he does not go so far as to reject along with Tradition II also Tradition I; whether he does not reject along with the authority of the Pope, the authority of the Church as the only realm within which the Scriptures are properly understood. [7]

The skepticism to which the private right to interpret the Bible may lead is well worded by Caspar Schwenckfeld (*ca.* 1530): "The Papists damn the Lutherans; the Lutherans damn the Zwinglians . . . ; the Zwinglians damn the Anabaptists and the Anabaptists damn all others." [8]

Luther is keenly aware of the threat of individualism; he protests that the hermeneutical principle should not be found in the individual listener or reader, but in Scripture itself: "Therein God is most interested that his Holy Word is purely preserved from additional teaching by man. But this Word cannot survive unless

[6] *Evangelium von den zehn Aussätzigen,* 1521; WA, 8, 341.

[7] It is George Tavard's contention that Luther replaced the authority of the Church with an arbitrary principle of his own liking. He would even boast in "my own doctrine" as Tavard repeats five times. See Tavard's *Holy Writ or Holy Church: The Crisis of the Protestant Reformation* (New York, 1960), pp. 81–96. Joseph Lortz defines Luther's position as "ein starker Dogmatismus im Subjektivismus, ein subjektiver Dogmatismus" (*Die Reformation in Deutschland,* Bd. I [2. Aufl.; Freiburg, 1941], S. 401). Albert Ebneter ("Luther und das Konzil," *Zeitschrift für katholische Theologie,* LXXXIV (1962), 19, Anm. 122) indicates the first passages where Luther comments on Augustine's *Ego non crederem:* WA, 2.429–32; 2.288; cf. 2.263. Tavard's conclusion should be compared with Ebneter's statement, "Das Urteil über die Wahrheit steht bei den Theologen, die in der Schrift ihr Fundament haben" (*art. cit.,* S. 13).

[8] *Corpus Schwenckfeldianorum* (Leipzig, 1907–61), Vol. IV, p. 818; quoted by Paul L. Maier, *Caspar Schwenckfeld on the Person and the Work of Christ* (Assen, 1959), p. 29.

one sees Christ as the sole *Bauherr* [master builder] and acknowledges him as such. If that is missing, unity is absent and Babel the
necessary result." [9]

Two years later Luther stresses the point that this understanding
of Christ as *Bauherr* is handed down by the Church (and for
Luther that means by the visible Church): "It [the Christian
Church] is the mother that begets and bears every Christian
through the Word of God. . . . ; where Christ is not preached,
there is no Holy Spirit to create, call, and gather the Christian
Church, and outside it no one can come to the Lord Christ." [10]

In 1528 in a treatise on rebaptism, Luther makes very clear that
his interpretation of the *sola Scriptura* principle does not exclude,
but includes, a high regard for Tradition I: "We do not act as
fanatically as the sectarian spirits. We do not reject everything
that is under the dominion of the Pope. For in that event we
should also reject the Christian Church. . . . Much Christian
good, nay, all Christian good, is to be found in the papacy and
from there it descended to us." [11]

This "descent" is the tradition of the living Word, of the same
Word which is contained in Holy Scripture, yet in a different
mode. There are not two sources for Christian Faith, but two
modes in which it reaches the Church in every generation: Holy
Scripture and the *viva vox evangelii*. This position would not be
restricted to that of Luther but would form a constitutive part of
the "heritage of the Reformation." The Calvinist *Confessio Helve-
tica posterior* (1562) would succinctly formulate this with the
words, *praedicatio verbi dei est verbum dei*: the preaching of the
word of God is *the* word of God.[12]

---

[9] 1527; WA, 24.233.
[10] 1529; *Large Catechism*, II, 3 (*Book of Concord*, edited by T. G. Tappert
[Philadelphia, 1959], p. 416). One wonders how Tavard could feel that it is
typical only of Calvinism that "in an inseparable diptych the Word guarantees
the Spirit, and the Spirit is the criterion of the Word" (*op. cit.*, p. 99).
[11] WA, 26.146–7.
[12] Caput I, i; in E. F. K. Mueller, *Die Bekenntnisschriften der reformierten
Kirche* (Leipzig, 1903), S. 171. For the understanding of Tradition in the
sixteenth century see J. N. Bakhuizen van den Brink, *Traditio in de Reformatie
en het Katholicisme in de zestiende Eeuw* (Amsterdam, 1952). For Melanchthon, see the very important dissertation by Peter Fraenkel, *Testimonia patrum:*

100

IV.

While the Reformation understood the co-inherence of Scripture and Church in terms of Tradition I, the Council of Trent in its fourth session gave its sanction to the co-inherence of Scripture and Church in terms of Tradition II. Herewith it finalized a development which we sketched above. Christian Faith reaches the Church in every generation through two sources, written and unwritten Tradition. The extra-scriptural Apostolic Tradition should be regarded with "equal esteem and loving respect" as the canonized written Tradition, Holy Scripture. This implies not only the coinciding of the *successio fidei* with the *successio episcoporum,* but also the elevation of the authority of the Church above the authority of the canonized Apostolic *kerygma.* Due to the restrictive localization of the *testimonium internum* of the Holy Spirit in the teaching office of the Church, Holy Scripture can only have a mute authority.[13]

Here we should mention Josef Geiselmann's effort to reinterpret this decision of the Council of Trent in such a sense that it really would have abstained from a decision in favor of Tradition II;[14]

The Function of the Patristic Argument in the Theology of Philip Melanchthon (Geneva, 1961). For Chemnitz and early Lutheranism, see Jaroslav Pelikan, "Die Tradition im konfessionellen Luthertum," *Lutherische Rundschau,* VI (1956–7), 228 sqq.; *Lutheran World,* III (1956), 214–22. And see my "Reformation, Preaching, and *Ex Opere Operato,*" in *Christianity Divided: Protestant and Roman Catholic Theological Issues,* edited by Daniel J. Callahan, Heiko A. Oberman, and Daniel J. O'Hanlon, S.J. (New York, 1961), pp. 223–39.

[13] The Reformation position is most succinctly stated by the Reformed theologian, Johannes Wollebius: "Testimonium hoc duplex est, principale et ministeriale. Principale est testimonium spiritus sancti,—ministeriale vero testimonium est testimonium ecclesiae" (*Christianae theologiae compendium* [Basel, 1526], p. 3; quoted by Heinrich Heppe–Ernst Bizer, *Die Dogmatik der evangelisch-reformierten Kirche* [neuarb. Aufl.; Neukirchen, 1958], S. 23).

[14] "Das Konzil von Trient über das Verhältnis der Heiligen Schrift und der nicht geschriebenen Traditionen," in M. Schmaus, *Die mündliche Ueberlieferung* (Munich, 1957), S. 125–206; esp. S. 148 sqq. For a more detailed presentation of the "Roman View," see J. K. S. Reid, *The Authority of Scripture* (New York, n. d.), pp. 121–44; Mr. Reid omits, however, a discussion of the "new theology" group.

Fr. Tavard has followed suit: the two sources theory results from the fact "that the main post-Tridentine theologians misinterpreted the formula of the Council." [15] The Council itself implicitly accepted the sufficiency of Holy Writ and understood Tradition as the *viva vox evangelii*. "For the opposite conception, that the Gospel is only partly in Scripture and partly in the tradition, was explicitly excluded." [16]

Though Geiselmann's interpretation has not remained uncontested,[17] it has been generally well received by Roman Catholic historians and theologians.[18]

We shall simply enumerate a series of considerations which make it impossible to accept Geiselmann's thesis.

(a) The partly-partly (*partim-partim*) formula of the original draft of the Tridentine decree on the respective authorities of Scripture and Tradition cannot be explained away as a product of

[15] *Op. cit.*, p. 244.

[16] *Op. cit.*, p. 208.

[17] Cf. H. Lennerz, "Scriptura sola?" *Gregorianum*, XL (1959), 38–53; "Sine scripto traditiones," *ibid.*, 624–35; Johannes Beumer, "Die Frage nach Schrift und Tradition bei Robert Bellarmin," *Scholastik*, XXXIV (1959), lieferungen," *Theologie und Glaube*, LI (1961), 161–80. See also Hubert Jedin, a scholar who is without doubt the greatest living authority on the Council of Trent: "Es kann nicht zweifelhaft sein, dass die Mehrzahl der in Trient anwesenden Theologen wenn nicht den Ausdruck partim-partim, so doch die Sache billigten, nämlich *dass die dogmatische Tradition einen die Schrift ergänzenden Offenbarungsstrom beinhalte*" (*Geschichte des Konzils von Trient*, Bd. II [Freiburg, 1957], S. 61).

[18] See *Herder Korrespondenz*, VIII (1959), 351: "Nach den Prinzipien katholischer Theologie und Kanonistik [würde] derjenigen Auffassung der Vorzug zu geben sein, die weniger in das Trienter Glaubensgesetz hineingelegt, und das ist die von Geiselmann." Cf. Peter Lengsfeld (*Ueberlieferung: Tradition und Schrift in der evangelischen und katholischen Theologie der Gegenwart* [Paderborn, 1960], S. 126) who tries to reconcile the points of view of Geiselmann, Lennerz, and Beumer. See, however, Lennerz, "Scriptura et traditio in decreto 4. sessionis Concilii Tridentini," *Gregorianum*, XLII (1961), 517–22. On grounds of the continued debate regarding the choice between "simili" and "pari" as adjectives for "affectu," Lennerz concludes (p. 521): "Manifestat Concilium mentem suam non mutavisse." Critical of Lennerz and favoring Geiselmann is Karl Rahner, *Ueber die Schriftinspiration* (Freiburg, 1959), S. 42 sqq., 80 sqq.

nominalistic philosophy as Geiselmann suggests.[19] Though one has
to cede to the nominalistic theologians the honor of having made
the two-source theory ripe for its official reception at Trent, the
formulation "partly-partly" as such is rare and has not yet been
traced to a Nominalist theologian. The more current translation of
the phrase of St. Basil, "some—and others" (*quasdam—quasdam*),
is used by Gabriel Biel but it can be traced back to the early
mediaeval canonists. In view of this textual history, one would be
well advised not to give too much weight to the change of the
initial "partly-partly" to the copulative "and" (*et*). All three formulations render St. Basil's own choice of words (*ta men, ta de*)
satisfactorily.

(b) This conclusion is borne out by the statement of the Cardinal Legate, Cervini, who announced on 6th April, 1546, after a
night spent on the revision of the original draft that the final
version is "in substance" the same.[20] This would hardly seem compatible with the idea that the Council changed its mind.

(c) The energetic protest against the "partly-partly" formulation which Geiselmann cites as the cause for the alleged change
proves to be limited to two representatives, Bonuccio and Nac-
chianti, of whom the first stands under suspicion of heresy on
points related to Scripture and Tradition and the second was once
called "avid for novelties." [21]

(d) The *Catechismus Romanus* (1566) quite clearly interprets
"and" (*et*) as "partly-partly" (*partim-partim*) when it states that
the Word of God is *distributed* over Scripture and Tradition.[22]

[19] "Das Konzil," S. 148, 177.
[20] Changes have been made, *"non tamen in substantia"* (*Concilium Tri-
dentinum* [Freiburg, 1901 sqq.], V, 76 [Henceforth, CT.]).
[21] CT, I, 535, 494. Cf. Spindeler, "Pari pietatis affectu," S. 171-2.
[22] "Omnis autem doctrinae ratio, quae fidelibus tradenda sit, verbo Dei
continetur, quod in scripturam, traditionesque distributum est" (Praefatio,
Sectio 12, *Catechismus Romanus ex decreto sacrosancti Concilii Tridentini
iussu S. Pii V Pontificis Maximi editus* [Rome, 1796], pp. 7-8). This *partim-
partim* is of course compatible with *et* whenever one speaks about Scripture
and Tradition as two sources of proof and confirmation: "Ac de huius quidem
doctrinae veritate [ignis purgatorius], quam et Scripturarum testimoniis, et
Apostolica traditione confirmatam esse sancta Concilia declarant . . ." (De
quinto articulo, Caput VI, 3, p. 59). Cf. *De Ordinis Sacramento*, Caput VII,
29, p. 325.

In short, the Council of Trent clearly admits that not all doctrinal truths are to be found in Holy Scripture. Tradition is seen as a second doctrinal source which does not "simply" unfold the contents of Scripture, as in Tradition I but, adding its own substance, complements the content of Holy Scripture. The gradually eroded connection between explicit and implicit truths has been snapped; the exegetical tradition has been transformed into Tradition II.

We have gone into some detail in order to present the historical background and setting of the doctrinal decision taken at the Council of Trent and not merely to refute Geiselmann's interpretation. Yet, however important it may be to try to set the historical record straight, we have to take Geiselmann's effort seriously as a theological expression representing a large and influential section of contemporary Roman Catholic theology. The position of this group can perhaps be best characterized by the adage, "The total [kerygma] is in Holy Scripture and at the same time in the unwritten traditions." [23]

Geiselmann is seriously concerned to show the fallacy of the two-source theory. But, as we shall see, this does not mean that he comes closer to an understanding of Tradition in terms of Tradition I.

V.

Let us now indicate a few landmarks which help us to find our way in the history of Roman Catholic thought on the relation of Scripture and Tradition from Trent to our own day. It is of course largely a history of the effort to interpret the mind of the Council on this point. [24]

The authority of the Roman catechism and the wide influence

---

[23] "Totum in sacra scriptura et iterum totum in sine scripto traditionibus . . ." (Geiselmann, "Das Konzil," S. 206).

[24] For the post-Tridentine period see: J. R. Geiselmann, *Die lebendige Ueberlieferung als Norm des christlichen Glaubens dargestellt im Geiste der Traditionslehre Johannes Ev. Kuhn* (Freiburg, 1959); Henri Holstein, *La Tradition dans l'Eglise* (Paris, 1960), p. 103–40; Yves M.-J. Congar, O.P., *La Tradition et les traditions*, T. I (Paris, 1960), p. 233–63.

of Peter Canisius and Robert Bellarmine have preserved into our own time the Tradition II concept which we found to be the intention of the participants at the Council of Trent.

The Tübingen School of the first part of the nineteenth century, indebted as it was to Romanticism with its emphasis on the organic and universalistic nature of society, has become identified with the notion of "living tradition." Johann Adam Möhler in his *Symbolik* of 1832 presented Tradition as the Gospel living in the Church; not simply as a conservation of the original deposit of faith, but as a development of it.[25] Holy Scripture was for Möhler the matter; the Church, the life-giving form.[26]

As we follow the course of the last century we should note that the Vatican Council quoted the Tridentine formulation and implied that Trent taught two parallel sources of Revelation.[27] In the same year, 1870, in which papal infallibility was declared, J. B. Franzelin published his *De divina Traditione et Scriptura,* emphasizing the concept of active tradition and the importance of the succession of Doctores.[28]

The two notions of living development and binding authority of the teaching office of the Church to which Cardinal Newman and the systematic theologian Matthias Scheeben († 1888) contributed in the same century, together with the declaration of the dogmas of the immaculate conception of the Virgin Mary (1854), of the definition of papal infallibility (1870), and of the pronouncement of the bodily assumption of the immaculate Virgin (1950), have led in our time to a reconsideration of the relation of the magisterium as active tradition and the so-called sources of Revelation as objective tradition. Appearances notwithstanding, the debate on the relation of Scripture and extra-biblical tradition has lost some of its former urgency. A Tradition III concept is in

[25] *Symbolik oder Darstellung der dogmatischen Gegensätze der Katholiken und Protestanten* (2. Aufl.; Cologne, 1958), Bd. I, S. 412–48.
[26] "Hiernach lautet der Grundsatz der Katholiken: Du wirst dich der vollen und ungeteilten christlichen Religion nur in Verbindung mit ihrer wesentlichen Form, welche da ist die Kirche, bemächtigen" (*ibid.,* S. 426).
[27] Denzinger-Schönmetzer, *Enchiridion symbolorum* (Freiburg, 1963), N. 3006.
[28] Congar, *La Tradition,* I, 251: Franzelin's work has "largement determiné la théologie moderne"; cf. Holstein, *La Tradition,* p. 125 sqq.

105

the process of being developed by those who tend to find in the teaching office of the Church the one and only source of Revelation. Scripture and Tradition are then not much more than historical monuments of the past. In any case the papal encyclical *Humani generis* of 12th August, 1950, can still be understood in terms of Tradition II. According to this authoritative document, the teaching office of the Church is the *regula proxima veritatis* or immediate rule for faith.[29]

On this point, however, where we cross over into the area of present-day events, we have to terminate our historical survey.

VI.

We want to select three systematic observations, which transcend the level of historical investigation but which seem to us to be implied in the foregoing: (1) the significance of Tradition I for the Protestant understanding of canon and canonicity; (2) the basic contrast between Protestant and Roman Catholic scholarship; (3) the implications of the development from Tradition II to Tradition III in Roman Catholic theology.

(1) It is important for Protestants who want to participate seriously in the present-day dialogue on Scripture and Tradition to know that they have to handle the traditional battle cry of *sola Scriptura* with care and precision.

"Scripture alone" stands for the sufficiency of Holy Scripture. This sufficiency expresses not only a doctrinal quantitative perfection but also a spiritual qualitative perfection. This corresponds to a twofold response of the Church, the articles of Faith (*fides quae*) and the act of Faith (*fides qua*). It is this correspondence which is taken seriously in the concept of Tradition I.

The Reformers were more aware than their predecessors in Tradition I that a distinction between material and formal sufficiency of Holy Scripture may carry the dangerous connotation of contrast between the dead matter of Holy Scripture and the life-giving form of the Church. But they always emphasized this: the

[29] *Acta apostolicae sedis* (henceforth, AAS), XLII (1950), 567.

sufficiency of Holy Scripture in both its material and formal aspects can only function when Scripture is opened, that is, when Scripture is seen as the Book given to the Church which is gathered and guided by the Holy Spirit. The Holy Spirit as the principal Doctor uses the Church to lead the faithful into all truth, that is, from implicit to explicit truth, to open the Scriptures by his internal testimony; by the drawing up of confessions; but primarily and centrally by the preaching of the *kerygma,* which is the very Word of God. Since we have demonstrated the mutual interdependence of *sola Scriptura* and Tradition I we are in a position to reject two claims concerning the role of Scripture, one of Protestant and one of Roman Catholic origin.

The first claim is the current Protestant insistence that the canon should be regarded, at least in principle, as open and subject to growth since the concept of a closed canon would imply the infallibility of the early Church.[30] Is it not clear, however, that the concept of an open canon to which other truths can be added is exactly that concept of Tradition which we have been sketching in its development to Trent and the Vatican Council? Not Tradition I, but Tradition II operates with an open canon, open towards the overflow of Revelation in Tradition.

It seems equally indefensible to sacrifice the concept of a closed canon for fear of a theory of verbal inspiration of a Mormon-like Holy Book. The closing of the canon is a historical process, subject to historical investigation.

Whereas from the standpoint of Tradition II the formation of the canon is to be regarded as an approval or *creation* by the Church, Tradition I speaks in terms of *reception* of the canon by the Church. Oscar Cullmann has called the Church's acknowledgment of the canonical books an act of humility.[31] Indeed the Church thus acknowledged the necessity of an unambiguous authority amidst the confusing claims of pseudepigraphic literature and oral traditions. Those writings which we now know as the

[30] Karl Barth, *Kirchliche Dogmatik,* I/2 (Zurich, 1938), 532; more recently, Gerhard Ebeling, *Die Geschichtlichkeit der Kirche und ihrer Verkündigung als theologisches Problem* (Tübingen, 1954), S. 51.

[31] *Die Tradition als exegetisches und historisches und theologisches Problem* (Zurich, 1954), S. 45; *The Early Church* (London, 1956), pp. 87–98.

canonical books were received as sharing in the uniqueness of God's revelation in Jesus Christ. It is this unique character which is expressed and respected in the concept of the closed canon.

The second claim to which we referred comes from the Roman Catholic side. Protestantism has been accused of undermining the authority of the canon by carving out after the example of Luther a canon within the canon.[32] To answer this claim we should first say that it is less polemical and more appropriate to speak of a living center of Holy Scripture than of the canon within the canon.

There are at least four ways in which the idea of a canon within the canon can be shown to function without undermining the authority of Scripture. (a) Irenaeus[33] and Tertullian see Holy Scripture as the receptacle of the rule of truth or the role of Faith and mean by these expressions a series of historical acts of God which are in manifold ways reflected in Holy Scripture. (b) This nucleus is not only the historical kernel but also and at the same time the hermeneutical center of Holy Scripture from which the lines of interpretation are drawn. (c) A historical investigation would indicate that each era and generation has and lives with its own canon even in those communions where through the centuries the same lectionary is followed. The very choice of these lections constitutes a canon within the canon. (d) Luther's hermeneutical principle, *Was Christum treibet*, allows every generation in its unique historical situation to discover new treasures in Holy Scripture and to add these to those already handed down to her in the exegetical tradition of the Church.

(2) In the second place, the contrast between Tradition I and Tradition II has far-reaching consequences for Protestant and Roman Catholic biblical interpretation and the exploration of the history of Christian thought. Cooperation in these fields can be fruitful, but only when the differing doctrinal bases are under-

---

[32] Tavard, *Holy Writ*, p. 85. See also Lengsfeld, *Ueberlieferung* (S. 94): "Eine Grenze, die innerhalb eines Rahmens verschiebbar ist, bleibt auch dann nur eine verschiebbare Grenze; und mit ihrer normativen Kraft ist es aus."

[33] Damien van den Eynde, *Les normes de l'enseignement chrétien dans la littérature patristique des trois premiers siècles* (Paris, 1933), p. 187.

stood; and the basis for Roman Catholicism is of course the latest concept of the relation of Scripture and Tradition.

A Roman Catholic theologian wrote in 1950 as a comment on the dogmatization of the bodily assumption of the Virgin Mary: "The theological discussion of Mariological questions is indicative of the contemporary state of Catholic systematic theology. Since the definition of the Immaculate Conception, it employs a method which was before that time not usual. The weakness of proofs from Scripture and Tradition gave the teaching office of the Church as the *regula proxima fidei* a primary position which had of course its repercussion on the concept of dogma as such. Not upheld by the certainty of graspable evidence, it has again been more strongly placed in the realm of irrational faith." [34] This seems to me not an extreme statement; it points to another important contribution of nominalistic theology which first in the later Middle Ages prepared the Church for the reception of Tradition II, and now again for this new development of Roman Catholic doctrine.

Humani generis declared in 1950 that it is the task of theology to show in what way a doctrine defined by the Church is contained in the sources of faith: Scripture and Tradition.[35] The task of the Doctor, be he biblical scholar or Church historian, is to read the latest doctrinal decision back into his sources. From the vantage point of mediaeval history, we may say that what first was the vital teaching office of the Doctor of Scripture, standing together with the Bishop as custodian of the deposit of Faith, has now been transformed into the office of Apologete of the Teaching Office of the Church; the Doctor has become the *ancilla papae!*

Scheeben, perhaps guided by the 1854 definition of the Immaculate Conception, had at the end of the nineteenth century granted that, though all problem areas are touched upon in Holy Scripture, not all Catholic truths are contained in Holy Scripture. For the future it was even more significant that the development from

[34] T. A. Sartory, quoted by Hans Grass, *Die katholische Lehre von der Heiligen Schrift und von der Tradition* ("Quellen zur Konfessionskunde," Reihe A, Nr. 1; Lüneburg, 1954), S. 63, Anm. 29.
[35] AAS, XLII (1950), 568.

"explicit," to "implicit," and finally to "silent" is reflected in his thought along with the distinction between analytic and synthetic interpretation.[36]

Between analytic and synthetic interpretation of the biblical and ecclesiastical sources runs the demarcation line dividing Protestant and Roman Catholic scholarship. The "secular" codes of historical inquiry will retain an importance for the Protestant theologian which it has not for his Roman Catholic colleague. The interpretation of the decision of the Council of Trent may serve as an example.

We have argued on strictly analytical grounds that Geiselmann's interpretation of Trent is untenable. We should, however, not overrate the importance of this historical conclusion for our Roman Catholic partner. For him it is the prerogative of his church to interpret its own sources; the documents of the past are to be interpreted by the teaching office since this is the authoritative centre of the living tradition.[37] By adding now to the traditional analytic method the synthetic method of interpretation, the Tridentine decree cannot constitute an obstacle for the Church in accepting officially the thesis that everything is simultaneously contained in Scripture and in Tradition.

Once such a doctrine were officially defined, it would instantly become the task of the Roman Catholic theologian to support Geiselmann's interpretation of the Tridentine decrees. An under-

---

[36] "Sie [die Tradition] kann und soll *ebensowenig* wie die Heilige Schrift eine *materiell adequate* Quelle und eine formell vollkommene Regel des Glaubens sein" (*Handbuch der katholischen Theologie*, Bd. I: *Theologische Erkenntnislehre* [3. Aufl.; Freiburg, 1959], S. 171). "In der Tat enthält die Schrift die *meisten und wichtigsten* Lehren der Tradition . . . in der Schrift [sind] alle Gebiete der offenbarten Wahrheiten wenigstens berührt, und weitaus die meisten einzelnen Wahrheiten virtuell ausgesprochen oder doch angedeutet so dass es *keine* offenbarte Wahrheit gibt, die nicht analytisch oder synthetisch als nähere Bestimmung oder Entwicklung der in der Schrift enthalten Wahrheiten sich darstellte und in dieser einen Anknüpfungspunkt finden könnte" (*ibid.*, S. 149). Peter Lengsfeld's study on Tradition is an example of this new apologetic task of the *Doctor* which should not be confused with historical inquiry. Omitting sections of the above quotations, he claims that Scheeben belongs to those who hold "das Enthaltensein aller Heilswahrheiten in der Schrift" (*Ueberlieferung*, S. 122, Anm. 140).

[37] "Totum depositum fidei . . . et custodiendum et tuendum et interpretandum concrederit [Magisterio]" (AAS, XLII [1950], 567).

standing of this basic difference as regards historical standards and method of interpretation between Roman Catholic and Protestant is a necessary condition for a realistic dialogue.

(3) Let us finally ask ourselves whether this new emphasis on the fact that everything is contained in Holy Scripture signifies a *rapprochement* to the Protestant position. It seems to me that the theological vision which stands behind Geiselmann's historical inquiry suggests that Tradition II has developed into Tradition III rather than that it is in the process of being transformed into Tradition I, however "open" the discussion of this matter at Vatican II may appear.

Tradition II developed, as we have said, out of Tradition I when the theologians and canon lawyers discovered that all the truths actually held by the Church could not be found explicitly or implicitly in Holy Scripture. Especially due to the Mariological dogmas of 1854 and 1950, theologians have concluded once again that not only Scripture but now also Scripture and Tradition taken together are materially insufficient to support by simple explication these authoritative definitions. Scripture and Tradition are still held to be the *sources*, and the teaching office of the Church, the *norm* which preserves and interprets the sources.[38] But inasmuch as this interpretation is synthetic, the norm takes on the function of the source. The Apostolic Constitution in which the bodily assumption of the Virgin Mary is defined refers to the unique consensus, not of the Church of all ages, but of the present-day Church. Not as an *argument for*, but as *part of*, this authoritative definition it is announced that this divine truth is contained in the deposit of Faith.

Whereas in Tradition I truth is grasped and held through reflection on Holy Scripture and in Tradition II through reflection [39] on Scripture and Tradition, in this last stage, the stage of Tradition III, truth is grasped and held by introspection and self-analysis on the part of the Church focused in the teaching office.

[38] Apostolic Constitution *Munificentissimus Deus* (November 1, 1950; AAS, XLII [1950], 757).

[39] Cf. Karl Barth, *Kirchliche Dogmatik*, I/2, 651.

The validity of our interpretation can perhaps be best documented by the words of the influential Roman Catholic theologian, Walter Burghardt: "A valid argument for a dogmatic tradition, for the Church's teaching in the past, can be constructed from her teaching in the present. And that is actually the approach theology took to the definability of the Assumption before 1st November, 1950. It began with a fact: the current consensus, in the Church teaching and in the Church taught, that the Corporeal Assumption was revealed by God. If that is true, if that is the teaching of the magisterium of the moment, if that *is* the Church's tradition, then it was always part and parcel of the Church's teaching, part and parcel of tradition." [40]

This state of affairs is certainly not promising for the Protestant-Roman Catholic dialogue. It would be unrealistic to deny this. Oscar Cullmann could end his important essay on Tradition with the encouraging observation that there is within Roman Catholicism a rising tide of interest in biblical studies proved by valuable Roman Catholic contributions to the understanding of Holy Scripture.[41] And, indeed, in the encyclical *Divino afflante Spiritu* of 30th September, 1943, a new era of Roman Catholic biblical studies was initiated.

But, in the light of the foregoing, we have to add that this upsurge of biblical research, welcome as it was to us, had to be realistically regarded as due to the movement away from the sources of Revelation to the norm of Revelation or, in other words, as due to the transformation of Scripture into a monument of the "living tradition."

Nevertheless, so long as the Roman Catholic Church was committed to Tradition II, it stood under the authority of its past decisions among which those of the Council of Trent formed a major barrier in the ecumenical dialogue. The Tradition III concept gives the Church a new and a large measure of freedom, not only over against Holy Scripture but also over against its own

[40] "The Catholic Concept of Tradition in the Light of Modern Theological Thought," *Proceedings of the Catholic Theological Society of America* (Washington, 1951), p. 74.
[41] *The Early Church*, p. 98.

doctrinal past. Although, therefore, Tradition III, does not imply a *rapprochement* to the Protestant position, it leaves room for the age-old dream so powerfully described by Friedrich Heiler, the dream of yearning for the "Evangelical Pope" [42] who would be able to break the bonds of tradition and guide the Roman communion back into obedience to the rule of Faith and full possession of the charism of truth.

SACRAMENTS

I.

It is not difficult to find a natural transition from our last topic "Tradition and Traditions" to a presentation of the Reformation view of the Sacraments. The question of the *number* of Sacraments comes immediately to mind: the Reformation confronted the mediaeval accumulation of seven Sacraments with the two Sacraments, Baptism and the Lord's Supper, instituted by Christ according to Holy Scripture. The point of this debate about the number of Sacraments in the sixteenth century and ever since has been, however, not primarily the nature of the Sacraments but the extent and validity of the Church's power to "develop" new Sacraments. This would not concern us here if there had not been a development of ecclesiology which has swung the pendulum back and traced the seven Sacraments to one *Ursakrament*. In the Vatican II Constitution on the Church it is first said (No. 1) that the Church is in Christ *veluti sacramentum* or as sign and instrument of the intimate union with God and of the unity of the whole human race. And again (No. 9) it is said that God constituted for all and everyone the Church as the *sacramentum visibile* of the saving unity in Christ.[1]

[42] Friedrich Heiler, *Der Katholizismus, seine Idee und seine Erscheinung* (2. Aufl.; Munich, 1923), S. 334.

[1] The official text reference is to Cyprian, *Epistula* LXIX, 6; Migne, *Patrologia Latina* (henceforth, PL), III, 1142: "The inseparable sacrament of unity."

In connection with what we have said about the proclivity of the *filioque* to extend into an *ecclesiaque*, it might be important to stress that the designation of the Church as *Ursakrament* does not contradict or invalidate the mediaeval developments but rather provides for its confirmation. The Church thus becomes the ground of being of all other Sacraments. But if we define Sacrament as the hidden but real presence of the Kingdom and Kingship of God in Christ, proclaimed by the Word, seen in Faith, it would have considerable advantages to refer rather to Jesus Christ as the *Ursakrament*,[2] if we want to use this category at all. In Jesus Christ the Kingdom received its *pied à terre*; in him the Kingdom is really present. With its participation in the Sacraments, the Church acknowledges and celebrates the fact that neither the Crucifixion nor the Ascension put an end to God's kingdom on earth, that, incorporated in him by Baptism and in the community gathered by him, we continue to have communion with him, rejoicing in the foretaste of the Kingdom. Through the Sacraments the Faith of the Christian is strengthened by these signs of God's sovereignty, the antidotes against all contrary signs which proclaim that God is overcome and dead.

The proposed new Presbyterian Confession, the so-called "Confession of 1967," articulates this context of the Sacraments excellently: "Biblical visions and images of the rule of Christ such as a heavenly city, a father's house, a new heaven and earth, a marriage feast, and an unending day culminate in the image of Kingdom. The Kingdom represents the triumph of God over all that resists his will and disrupts his creation. Already God's reign is present as a ferment in the world, stirring hope in men and preparing the world to receive its ultimate judgment and redemption."[3]

As the first of a series of points in this position paper, I should like to observe that when we refer to Jesus Christ as the *Ursakrament* we do not only want to express the truth that the Sacraments are the reflections of God's presence in Jesus Christ "recon-

[2] Cf. Augustine: "Non est enim aliud Dei sacramentum nisi Christus" (*Epistula* CLXXXVII, 34; PL, XXXVIII, 845).
[3] Part III, "The Fulfillment of Reconciliation," *Presbyterian Life*, May 1, 1965, p. 39.

ciling the world with himself." That is the incarnational aspect which should indeed be taken into consideration but not in isolation. If isolated, it would imply a description of God in terms of being (as, for instance, is the case with the doctrine of transubstantiation as an interpretation of divine presence in the Eucharist). God is not only present in Jesus Christ according to the confession of the Church; he is also acting in Jesus Christ. There is a *history* of God in Jesus Christ reflected here which should be traced through to the Ascension. It gives the Sacraments a world-wide perspective, articulates the distance between the Church and the Kingdom and lends to history as such the character of Sacrament. If the Incarnation as one phase or event in this history is chosen as the point of reference, some kind of doctrine of "substantiation" results. If the Passion and Crucifixion is one-sidedly emphasized, Baptism becomes the locus of contrition and the Eucharist becomes a memorial service. If the Resurrection becomes the central point of reference Baptism becomes a condition for life eternal and the Eucharist the *pharmakon athanasias*.

We said above that the history of Jesus Christ should be traced through to the Ascension; it would perhaps be more in keeping with the structure of the theological enterprise to assume the backward stance. From the point of view of our common expectation of the coming of Christ in glory and of his appearance in complete visibility when every knee will bow before him, from the point of view of our common faith in Christ's rule at the right hand of the Father, we look back on that part of the *magnalia Dei* that have already taken place in the Old Testament, in the New Testament, and in subsequent history.

To emphasize the Ascension as the appropriate point of departure for a truly Catholic understanding of the Sacraments does not mean that one neglects or denies the partial truth gleaned from looking in turn towards the Incarnation, Passion, Crucifixion, and Resurrection. But each next event in the history of Jesus Christ sheds its own light and interprets the preceding event. The divine "necessity" Christ referred to when he said to his former disciples on the road to Emmaus, "Was it not necessary that the Christ should suffer these things and enter into his glory?" (Lk. 24:26), is

115

not to be confused with historical causation or rational predictabil-
ity. The Anselmian "necessary reasons," the *rationes necessariae*
according to which the Incarnation and Crucifixion can be proved,
are only acceptable from the backward stance of the *fides quaerens
intellectum.*

The pattern of necessity which Faith discerns in the *magnalia
Dei* is the faithfulness of the Covenant-God who does not "abandon the works of his hand" (Ps. 138:9). In the light of the Passion
and Crucifixion, the royal *introitus* and Virgin Birth of Christmas
receive the sobering Pauline connotation: "born from a woman,
born under the law" (Gal. 4:4). The Resurrection in turn shows
that the Cross is not the end of another messianic dream or the
terminal point of a human tragedy. Through the Resurrection the
Cross is seen as the unexpected form or mode of the eschatological
rule of God, of Christian existence and thought.

If we regard the history of Christ as the *Ursakrament,* as the
visible sign of the coming Kingdom, we should note that the death
of Christ on Calvary was visible to all but the empty tomb was
visible only to the eyes of Faith. In the same way, water, wine, and
bread are visible signs of the coming Kingdom yet visible only
when seen in Faith, certified by the Word. In this sense the
Augustinian saying, *Verbum accedit ad elementum et fit sacramentum* (the Word comes to the element and makes the Sacrament), has become fundamental for the Reformation understanding of Sacrament.

But we are not allowed to stop here. The Resurrection is again
unpredictably interpreted by the Ascension. The radical reversal of
what man had come to regard as natural law, as the law of the
flesh, of time and death, leads over into the time of patience
(Barth) or of the divine *epoche* (Van Ruler). Only in the setting
of a theological dualism can we note that the divine offensive,
seemingly grinding to a halt, has taken another unexpected move
and advance.

The two speeches of the Apostle Peter in Acts (2:14 sqq. and
3:19 sqq.) reveal this *epoche* and change in the eschatological
timetable. Peter quotes Joel 2:28: "And it shall come to pass
afterward that I will pour out my spirit on all flesh." Peter quotes

Joel faithfully except that the events described by Joel are now spread out over a period of time by adding "in these last days." [4] There is an *epoche* and surprise that the coming of the Christ and the victory over death have not brought us further than that we dream dreams: the realization of these dreams is still outstanding. This *epoche* comes through again as "the time of God's patience" in the second speech of Peter: "Repent and turn again so that your sins may be blotted out in order that times of refreshment may come from the face of the Lord and that *he may send the Messiah which is appointed for you,* Jesus, whom heaven must receive *until the times of ultimate consummation,* concerning which times God spoke through the mouth of the Holy Prophets." The witness of the Old Testament is here related to the *Parousia,* which we usually call the *second* coming.[5]

According to the Qumran community—and actually according to all Jews except the Sadducees—resurrection and these "times of refreshment" belong together. In the Christian timetable the two have been unexpectedly separated to create the time of patience, the era of the Ascension, the time of the Church, time for the world. The wider perspective of this "time for the world" was preserved by the Church Fathers when they used the word "mystery" to designate the ongoing action of God in history.[6] In a more specific way the word "mystery" came to refer to the Sacraments, the marks of the era of the Ascension.

The Reformation theology of the Sacraments in its various expressions can only be understood as a reinterpretation of the nature of the Sacraments in the light of God's *epoche* in the Ascension era. In and around the Sacraments the basic petition of the Lord's Prayer is granted: his rule is established, his name sanctified on earth as it is already in heaven where Christ sits at the right hand of the Father. For this reason the marks of the Church were, *inter alia,* seen in the right administration of the

[4] See on this matter Arnold A. van Ruler, *De Vervulling van de Wet* (Nykerk, 1947), blz. 132–3.

[5] Krister Stendahl finds in this section "the ring of a very original type of messianology—or christology" (*The Scrolls and the New Testament* [New York, 1957], p. 14).

[6] W. C. van Unnik, *Oratio catechetica* (Amsterdam, 1949), blz. 55 sqq.

Sacraments, and for this reason one is inclined from the point of view of the Reformation tradition to opt rather for Christ than for the Church as the *Ursakrament*.

II.

We can now turn to two Latin phrases which still retain their central place in the discussion of the Sacraments in the *ecclesia catholica reformata: praesentia realis* and *ex opere operato*. In a recent article Bishop Willem Bekkers said: "The Church retains unwaveringly her doctrine of the real presence. . . . But how we have to think about this real presence is not prescribed by the Church."[7] It is a question of historical inquiry whether the Roman Catholic Church has not designated transubstantiation as the prescribed form of understanding the real presence of Christ in the Eucharist. The Council of Trent teaches that Christ is not only *realiter* but also *substantialiter* present under the species of bread and wine.[8] In a special chapter, "De Transubstantiatione," it reaffirmed the teaching of the Fourth Lateran Council when it stated that the conversion is *convenienter et proprie* called *transubstantiatio*.[9]

On many accounts this formulation was unacceptable to the Reformers. It implies the Church's *imprimatur* upon a particular philosophy; insofar as the term suggests an analogy with the Incarnation, it presupposes a heretical Christology, namely, that of Docetism according to which Christ only *appeared* from the outside to be a real man; but above all it is related to the divorce of consecration and communion, to the division between *praesentia* and *usus*. The dissociation of consecration and communion expressed in the reservation of the Host may be understandable in the context of the history of devotion, but the Western doctrinal development formulated in the adage *lex orandi est lex credendi*

[7] *Analecta*, March, 1965; quoted by J. Arts, "Een Jaar Eucharistie," *De Nieuwe Linie*, 15 Mei, 1965, blz. 12 (my own translation).

[8] Denzinger-Schönmetzer, *Enchiridion symbolorum*, N. 1636 (N. 874, former editions).

[9] *Ibid.*, N. 1642 (N. 877, former editions).

warns us to take this devotional practice very seriously theologically. If I am right in my assessment of the *théologie nouvelle* as reaching far into the episcopal ranks, which the words of Bishop Bekkers during the sessions of the Second Vatican Council would indicate, the defense of transubstantiation is being abandoned for new and as yet unclear ways of articulating the real presence.

A parallel development can be observed on the Reformation side of discussion on the Eucharist. In the consensus of 1956 on the Lord's Supper between the Netherlands Reformed Church and the Evangelical Lutheran Church in the Netherlands [10] and in the documents related to the Arnoldhainer Theses of 1957, the proposed consensus between Lutherans and Reformed in Germany,[11] we note the same tendency to move away from a formulation of the mode of the presence and towards a description of the purpose of the presence as redemptive, looking towards the *Parousia*, and constitutive of the Church. In both consensuses one is struck by the emphasis upon the dynamic nature of the celebration of the Sacrament as event and upon the communion as *communio sanctorum* rather than upon the communion of the individual.

It is not a sign of romantic optimism to find here the possibility of *rapprochement* within the Western tradition. But as regards the issue of the eucharistic sacrifice, no such optimism is permissible. Together with the real presence Luther and Calvin spoke about the sacrifice of praise and thanksgiving, and the Latin word *memoria* used by the Reformers has the deep mystical connotation of *anamnesis* rather than that of a psychological representation of the past. But this personal and communal identification with the sacrifice of Christ is seen from the point of view of Abelard instead of that of Anselm, the sacrifice of God in Christ as directed towards the faithful instead of the sacrifice of Christ to God, since the substitutionary sacrifice on Calvary took place once and for all. A recovery of *memoria* as link between past and future and,

[10] C. W. Monnich en G. C. Van Niftrik, *Hervormd-Luthers Gesprek over het Avondmaal* (Nykerk, 1958).

[11] *Zur Lehre vom heiligen Abendmahl*, herausgegeben von G. Niemeier (Munich, 1959); *Lehrgespräch über das heilige Abendmahl*, herausgegeben von G. Niemeier (Munich, 1961); *Kirche und Abendmahl*, herausgegeben von V. Vajta (Berlin, 1963).

together with that, an understanding of the *anamnesis* of the whole history of Christ extending to the Ascension point the way for future ecumenical dialogue. It is important for us to move from a fruitless discussion of the relation of the two sacrifices—Calvary and the altar—towards an understanding of the Sacraments in general and of the Eucharist in particular in the context of a theological dualism, as I suggested in my first paper. This means the Sacraments are regarded as the signs of the disintegration of the Kingdom of Evil and its hold on creation, the cracks through which the coming Kingdom of God is breaking in. Around the Sacraments the unique features of the Church become visible as the community of believers who have foresworn the devil and his *pompa*, who participate through Baptism in the death and resurrection of their head in the Eucharist, who receive a foretaste of the full visibility of the sovereignty of God, and who look forward to the *Parousia* of the ascended Lord.

III.

It is difficult to establish historically whether the dissociation of consecration and communion was due to the increasing liturgical emphasis upon the Eucharist as sacrifice or whether the sacrificial interpretation of the Eucharist together with the growth of private Masses drew all attention to consecration and elevation. The crux of discussion of the sacrifice of the Mass from the sixteenth century till our own day seems to me related to the term *ex opere operato* and this in turn to a false view of the relation of the two Testaments. It might be well for us to turn to a concise statement on the Sacraments by the Council of Florence, not only because this council was concerned with the division between the Eastern and Western branches of the Church but also because it gave a short summary of the understanding of the Sacraments on the eve of the Reformation which would set the stage of the later Rome-Reformation debate.

In the *Bulla* "Exsultate Deo" of November 22, 1439, we read: "To make it more easy to instruct the Armenians of the present day as well as those to come, we summarize the true nature of the Sacraments of the Church in the following brief formula. There are seven Sacraments of the New Law, namely Baptism, Confirmation, the Eucharist, Penance, Extreme Unction, Ordination and Marriage. These differ very much from the Sacraments of the Old Law. After all, those did not cause grace, but foreshadowed the grace that was only to be granted through the passion of Christ. Our Sacraments, however, not only contain grace, but also confer it on those who receive them worthily." [12]

In canon 8 of the Tridentine Decree on the Sacraments, promulgated March 3, 1547, this transmission of grace by the Sacraments is spelled out as *ex opere operato:* "If anyone says that through the Sacraments of the New Law grace is not conferred *ex opere operato* but that faith alone in the divine promise suffices to receive grace, *anthema sit.*" [13] According to Scholastic theology *ex opere operato* is the expression of the thesis that the proper performance of a sacramental rite has objective effects independent of the subjective condition of the priest and the participants.

It has long been assumed that *ex opere operato* is typical of the Roman Catholic doctrine of the Sacraments, so much so that it could become the slogan of anti-Roman publications and the battle cry of Roman Catholic denunciations of the Reformation tradition. However, insofar as *ex opere operato* stands for a rejection of Donatism, the term is indicative of the common basis of Roman Catholic and Protestant theology. In its anti-Donatist thrust *ex opere operato* indicates that the effect of the administration of a Sacrament is independent of the dignity of the administrant. Since the fourth century the Church has rejected the claim of the Donatists that the clergy should at least be holy men. The Reformation, on the whole very sensitive to the sovereignty of God, agreed that human weakness and sin in the administering clergyman could not form an obstacle to God's operation. None of the Reformers put this more eloquently than Luther: "Although a

[12] Denzinger-Schönmetzer, *Enchiridion symbolorum*, N. 1310 (N. 695, former editions); also contained in the excellent edition by John H. Leith, *Creeds of the Churches* (New York, 1963), p. 60.
[13] Denzinger-Schönmetzer, *ibid.*, N. 1608 (N. 851, former editions).

rascal, a godless and unbelieving person takes or gives the Sacrament, he takes or gives the true Sacrament . . . just as truly as he who administers and receives it most worthily. For the Sacrament is not based on the holiness of man but on the word of God." [14] And Calvin can say: "The power of the mystery remains intact no matter how much wicked men may try their utmost to nullify it." [15]

In the sense of the Tridentine contrast between *ex opere operato* and Faith, the joint Reformation tradition has indeed unanimously rejected *ex opere operato*. One of the factors at stake here is, of course, the difference in understanding the nature of Faith. In the wide variety of views ranging from the Nominalist, Robert Holcot († 1349), to the Thomist, Thomas de Vio or Cajetanus († 1532), devotion and faith are acknowledged as conditions for worthy and fruitful participation. Trent is rejecting *sola fides* as the sufficient subjective condition in the participants or *adstantes*.

Another—in this context more serious—factor was the mediaeval connection between *ex opere operato*, *signum efficax* and *causa gratiae*. When Trent says that the Sacraments confer grace *ex opere operato* upon all those who do not place an obstacle in its way (*non ponentibus obicem*), the necessity of devotion and faith is minimalized in order to underscore the objective causality of the Sacraments. Perhaps under the influence of the Dominican, E. Schillebeeckx, modern Roman Catholic theology may be more inclined to discuss the Sacraments in relational categories such as "encounter." [16] The Rome-Reformation discussion of *ex opere operato* can be reopened if Schillebeeckx is followed in his interpretation of the term as the bringing about of "the actual encounter with Christ." [17] *Ex opere operato* can thus protect the real presence of Christ against a Pelagian emphasis on the necessity of human cooperation, parallel to the function of the doctrines of

[14] WA, 6.6770.

[15] *Institutes of the Christian Religion*, IV, xvii, 33; edited by John T. McNeill ("Library of Christian Classics," Vol. XXI; Philadelphia, 1960), p. 1406.

[16] *De sacramentele Heilseconomie* (Antwerp, 1952). For Schillebeeckx's first work in English translation, see "The Sacraments: An Encounter with God," in *Christianity Divided*, edited by Daniel J. Callahan, Heiko A. Oberman, and Daniel J. O'Hanlon, S.J., pp. 245–75.

[17] "The Sacraments," *ibid.*, p. 269.

predestination and irresistibility of grace in the area of Justification. At the moment, however, because *ex opere operato* is contrasted with Faith, Faith is reduced to a subjective quality in man rather than seen as the work of the Holy Spirit which bridges the realms of objectivity and subjectivity, thus making for a real encounter.[18] This notion of Faith enables Calvin to say: "Christ, when he illumines us into Faith by the power of his Spirit, at the same time so engrafts us into his body that we become partakers of every good." [19]

By way of conclusion we might point out that the unpneumatological (*entpneumatologosierte!*) interpretation of the Sacraments in Roman Catholicism is not due to a one-sided reaction against the Reformation emphasis on Faith, but has a longer history with whose elements we have to come to terms if we want to make any progress in the ecumenical dialogue. In our final comment we cannot do more than indicate three of them: The shift from *epiclesis* to consecration, the rejection of the Augustinian-Scotist grasp of the covenantal context of the Sacraments (*pactum cum ecclesia*) as occasionalism, the one-sided and therefore distorting contrast of the Sacraments of the Old Testament as efficacious merely *ex opere operantis*, on grounds of Faith, with the *ex opere operato* efficacy of the Sacraments of the New Testament. Of these three, the last may well be the most fundamental in that it, together with the *timor-amor* and Law-Gospel comparisons, reduces the Old Testament to a lower preparatory stage before the *real* history of salvation begins.

GRACE

I.

There are two layers in contemporary ecumenical discussion, not always easily distinguished or distinguishable, but both are important for our understanding of the doctrine of grace.

[18] See G. C. Berkouwer, *De Sacramenten* (Kampen, 1954), blz. 91.
[19] *Institutes*, III, ii, 35, in McNeill, *op. cit.*, p. 583. Cf. III, xi, 10 (in McNeill, *op. cit.*, p. 737) and the comments on the *unio mystica* by Gott-

There is, in the first place, the effort to bring the results of modern biblical and historical studies to bear on centuries-old confessional differences in the hope of destroying mutual caricatures and of discovering the essential barriers. Since biblical and historical studies are no longer undertaken in confessional isolation, systematic theologians can no longer limit their choice of biblical and historical authorities to spokesmen of their own tradition. Impressive examples of this development with respect to our topic of grace are Hans Küng's dissertation on Karl Barth's doctrine of justification [1] and, more self-critical (and therefore even more eloquent), the document published in connection with the fourth convention of the Lutheran World Federation at Helsinki in 1963.[2] These two studies are perhaps even more than examples of a changing climate; they suggest a new context for a discussion which has lasted as long as the Church itself.

Secondly, the quest for a bridge between "the Church in a world come of age" and that world is a dominant theme in the theology of our time. On the Protestant side, there are the "schools" of Rudolf Bultmann, Dietrich Bonhoeffer, Paul Tillich, and John A. T. Robinson, each building bridges by seeking to demythologize the Church, the World, or past efforts to relate the two.

Bishop Robinson describes the nature of the Church in a secular setting as "the accepting community." "The characteristic of such a community is that it is prepared to meet men *where they are,* accept them for what they are." [3] It is striking that the hard

---

fried W. Locher in his important contribution, *Testimonium internum: Calvins Lehre vom Heiligen Geist und das hermeneutische Problem* (Zurich, 1964), S. 23.

[1] *Rechtfertigung: Die Lehre Karl Barths und eine katholische Besinnung* (Einsiedeln, 1957); ET *Justification* (New York, 1964).

[2] *Rechtfertigung heute: Studien und Berichte* (Stuttgart, 1965), with selected bibliography (S. 81-4); ET *Justification Today* (Supplement to *Lutheran World*, XII [1965]). From the non-Lutheran Protestant side, mention should be made of the stimulating article by W. D. Davies, "Challenge to Dialogue in the New Testament," in *Ecumenical Dialogue at Harvard*, edited by S. H. Miller and G. E. Wright (Cambridge, Mass., 1964), pp. 110-51, and the very important study by G. C. Berkouwer, *The Second Vatican Council and the New Catholicism* (Grand Rapids, 1965).

[3] *The New Reformation* (Philadelphia, 1965), p. 46.

outline of the traditional Protestant doctrine of justification re-appears here in a description of the Church.

The basic difference between the Protestant and the Roman Catholic doctrines of justification and grace has often been described in just those terms: according to the Reformation, God justifies the sinner on man's level; according to Roman Catholic belief, God justifies the sinner on God's level. By this is meant that God's justice would be compromised if he should finally accept a man who had not, through the help of grace, become sanctified enough to be worthy of that divine acceptance. By justification of the sinner on the sinner's level is meant that God's justice is established precisely in his gracious acceptance of man as he is.

As the quotation from Bishop Robinson shows, the two layers about which we spoke converge. The first of these has an ortho-dox-conservative parentage, motivated primarily by a concern for the *preservation* of truth; the second has a liberal-progressive par-entage, motivated primarily by a concern for the *communication* of truth. Orthodox and liberal Christians, formerly in clearly defined camps, have now reached a point of interdependence which makes it difficult, if not inappropriate and offensive, to separate them.

Exactly the same development can be noted within Roman Catholicism. *Pacem in terris* and the Decree on Ecumenism are examples of bridge-building on the highest level of hierarchical authority. There are books such as John Courtney Murray's *We Hold These Truths* and Michael Novak's *The Open Church* and articles such as those of Gregory Baum in the *Ecumenist* which document the Roman Catholic search for the scope of God's plans in the world outside the Church, with the *salus extra ecclesiam*. Even a superficial reading of the literature on Vatican II shows how confusing it is to use as self-evident such ambiguous, two-layer, terms conservative and progressive.

We shall have each of these layers in mind when we turn to the yield of recent biblical and historical studies for our appreciation of the Reformation doctrine of grace and justification, and proceed thence to the question of whether the Reformation's position on this point can contribute to "the quest for a bridge."

II.

It is very often said with regard to the Protestant *sola Scriptura* that actually no Christian church is able to read and receive Scripture without tradition. Though this state of affairs does not diminish the importance of acknowledging the principle of the supreme authority of Holy Scripture as the *regula proxima et ultima veritatis* it does not require extensive research to discover that the Reformation churches have acquired their own layers of tradition, spread out over the pages of Scripture. Exactly for this reason is it so refreshing to discover that the Helsinki meeting mentioned above provides a fine example of the *sola Scriptura* principle being applied to the critical evaluation of Luther's theology and Lutheran confessional documents.

As one of three main points the concept *simul iustus et peccator* is subjected to such a critical inquiry. It is pointed out that though not verbally present, the idea itself is biblical. On the one hand, the past of the sinner has passed away into the past history of Christ; on the other hand, the redeemed Christian is not yet through with sin: the indicative and imperative are twin forms, intimately related. Yet a consciousness of sin, as a permanent attitude of repentance, seems to be foreign to the New Testament. "Thus the position of the baptized is not understood as one in which they sin on the one hand and do what is right on the other and so are *simultaneously* slaves of sin and righteousness. Rather, in the obedience of faith they are the slaves of God, freed from bondage to sin, but *at the same time* there is the danger of falling into the bondage of sin again by sinning and thus falling victim to death. So they are exhorted to present their members for the service of righteousness." [4]

In the second place, the relation of justification and Baptism came under discussion. The realization that these two belong together for Paul (1 Cor. 6:11; Rom. 10:9–10), that the biblical

[4] Nils A. Dahl, "In What Sense Is the Baptized Person 'simul justus et peccator' According to the New Testament?" *Lutheran World*, IX (1962), p. 228.

doctrine of justification does not allow for antinomianism: "Union with Christ in his death and resurrection is both the assurance and the ethical dynamic of the Christian." [5] Furthermore, the life of the justified sinner is a life in Christ and the new life is life in the *soma christou* (1 Cor. 12:13; Gal. 3:28). Justification through its bond with Baptism has a communal dimension which relates the saved sinner to the saved community.

This relation reappears in a recent consideration of Justification and the Last Judgment: "To be a member of the Church is by definition to be justified, and he who remains in the Church will be saved. If someone backslides, he will not be saved. . . . Thus the Last Judgment is one facet of the consummation, which the early Church, Paul included, looked forward to with reasonable assurance that it would become a very glorious and joyous day for them." [6]

The Helsinki document reflects these biblical considerations and says, in a vicarious confession of faith for world Protestantism: "Justification creates fellowship. The message of the Gospel is truncated, if it is limited to the individual and his seeking after God. This message embraces and renews the whole creation. The place where the justifying act of God takes place is the Church." [7] "The man who in baptism has received the justifying grace of God in Christ is thereby called to a new life. The power of the resurrection ought to be visible in his life. Faith should show itself in deeds of love." [8] "Through baptism we are taken into the death of Christ so that in his resurrection we may lead a new life. In Lutheranism the *cross* has become the center of the proclamation, but in consequence the message of the *resurrection* has to a large extent been pushed in the background. It has been forgotten that baptism embraces the whole life of the Christian." [9]

[5] Warren A. Quanbeck, "Justification and Baptism in the New Testament," *Lutheran World*, VIII (1961), p. 15.

[6] Krister Stendahl, "Justification and the Last Judgment," *Lutheran World*, VIII (1961), p. 7.

[7] Section 11 of the version of Assembly Document 75 slightly revised and approved by the Commission of Theology in Pullach, July 29–August 3, 1964; *Rechtfertigung heute*, S. 12; *Justification Today*, p. 7.

[8] *Ibid.*, Section 16; *Rechtfertigung heute*, S. 13; *Justification Today*, p. 6.

[9] *Ibid.*, Section 10.

My high regard for the Helsinki contribution to our ecumenical discussions can perhaps best be articulated by my saying that the biblical doctrine of justification has also been thoroughly applied to its formulation and choice of words to the extent that there is no shadow of ecclesial triumphalism in evidence.

III.

It was not the task of those involved in the Helsinki reports to pose the question whether Luther discovered the Gospel. Their assessment concerned rather the reception of Luther's heritage in subsequent centuries of Lutheranism. In the quest to rediscover the catholicity of the Reformation and for an ever new reformation movement towards the *ecclesia catholica reformata*, it cannot be of secondary importance to raise this very question.

We must realize that Luther, just as Zwingli and Calvin, understood his mission as the reformation of the *whole* mediaeval Church and it is that which forms therefore his sounding board. A direct confrontation of Luther's theology with Holy Scripture, the New Testament or St. Paul is necessary for the implementation of *sola Scriptura* as the guiding confessional principle for the Church today; it cannot, however, serve as the historical standard of evaluation of Reformation theology. If we limit our discussion here to Luther as the *Inceptor Venerabilis* and *Doctor Communis* in world Protestantism, it should be emphasized that Luther did not formulate eternal truths, repeat Holy Scripture, or just reiterate St. Paul. He spoke in the context of the mediaeval Western tradition and applied the *kerygma* to the intellectual and existential structures of his time.

For this very reason fidelity to the Reformation today does not mean that one reiterate statements of the Reformers. Rather, it means *historically* that, confronted by the same alternatives the Reformers had to face, one is willing to affirm the decision made then; *systematically* it means that one is willing to apply the *kerygma* as recaptured in the Reformation, to the intellectual and existential structures of *our* time.

In our final section we shall try to make some such systematic observations.

Here it should be noted, first of all, that it is disastrous for a true understanding of Reformation theology to divorce mediaeval and Reformation studies, institutionally formalized at many universities by establishing two separate chairs to deal with the development of intellectual and Christian thought in these two periods. This fundamental co-inherence of mediaeval and Reformation thought cannot be pursued here in any detail. We make an exception however for Luther's understanding of grace as it applies to justification and the Law.

It has been said by Roman Catholic historians that Luther's theology has to be understood as an appropriate attack on late-mediaeval theology, particularly on late-mediaeval Nominalism. However, since this movement is to be regarded as fundamentally un-Catholic or even anti-Catholic, he failed to come to grips with the fullness of the mediaeval Catholic heritage.[10] Luther's critique of a distorted doctrine of grace applies therefore, it is argued, to nominalistic theologians but not to the disciples of Thomas Aquinas and Duns Scotus. Such a presentation can in turn lead to the conclusion that the traditional Protestant rejection of the mediaeval doctrine of grace has to be traced back to a tragic, perhaps well-intended but disastrous, misunderstanding on the part of the early Reformers, especially Luther. As a matter of fact it is by no means unusual that at ecumenical encounters the thesis is proclaimed that this misunderstanding has now been cleared up. It is then argued that the doctrine of grace and justification is no longer a dogmatic barrier since not only Hans Küng and Karl Barth but also the Council of Trent and Luther's intentions can be reconciled.

An analysis of the relevant mediaeval sources establishes, however, that Luther not merely attacked one particular school, i.e., Nominalism, but that he rejected a position which Thomists,

[10] See my *Harvest of Medieval Theology* (Cambridge, Mass., 1963), pp. 423 sqq., and the survey article, "The Reformation in Recent Catholic Theology," by Erik Persson (*Dialog*, II [1963], pp. 24–31) which is conveniently accessible in *New Theology No. 1*, edited by Martin E. Marty and Dean G. Peerman (New York, 1964), pp. 94–108.

Scotists, Nominalists and the Fathers of Trent held in common. His discovery of the *iustitia Dei passiva*, justification by faith in Christ through the grace of the Holy Spirit, was not the assertion of the prevenience of grace. It had indeed this anti-Pelagian thrust, but if this would have been all it would not have been a "new" insight, since there had always been a mediaeval anti-Pelagian school of thought. Nor was this his discovery: the justified sinner personally appropriates the *iustitia Christi*, the righteousness of Christ, through the reception of sacramental grace. This had always been part of Thomist and Scotist teaching, and was to be reasserted at the Council of Trent.

The most concise and therefore perhaps most helpful description of the point which Luther wanted to make in bringing St. Paul to bear on the mediaeval tradition is his identification of the righteousness of Christ and the justice of God, of the *iustitia Christi* and the *iustitia Dei (activa)*. According to the tradition he confronted, the *iustitia Christi* is the process of justification, usually initiated, in any case sustained by the gift of grace or charity. But the gift of the *iustitia Christi* never does imply the gift of the *iustitia Dei*. The *iustitia Dei* remains the standard for the justified *viator*, the standard according to which the religious health and progress of the pilgrim on his way to the eternal Jerusalem is evaluated. The *iustitia Dei* remains the law according to which the fruits of the granted righteousness of Christ are to be tested on the day of judgment. This in turn explains the "fear and trembling" emphasis of Trent and its doctrine of the uncertainty of salvation. For Luther the essence of the Gospel is that the *iustitia Dei*, revealed on the Cross as the *iustitia Christi*, is granted to the faithful through Faith. The *fides Christo formata* [11] has taken the place of the *fides caritate formata* of Thomas, Scotus, Biel, and Trent.

In Mariology the terminology is slightly changed but the identity of structure is quite clear. In a *catena* of sermons on the Ascension of the Virgin Mary one encounters, from Bernard of Clairvaux on, the following pattern: Christ hears about the arrival of his mother in heaven, hastens to meet her and then offers to

[11] WA, 40. I. 229, 8 sq.

130

share with her the kingdom of his Father. She would rule the Kingdom of Mercy and thus become the *Mater Misericordiae*. He, Christ, would undertake the rule of justice in order to function as the *iudex vivorum et mortuorum*.[12] The terminology in the devotional literature is not always the same as in the dogmatic treatises but it is obvious that here the mercy of the Virgin and the justice of Christ play the same role as the gift of the righteousness of Christ over against the standard of the justice of God which I indicated above.

Another eloquent example of the indicated difference between Luther and the Scholastic-Tridentine tradition can be found in a beautiful All Saints Day sermon by Bernard of Clairvaux himself. As a comment upon Psalm 142 (143):2—"no living being shall be justified in thine sight"—Bernard observes that "living being" applies both to men and angels; but, he goes on to say, even the angels who live so much closer to God, are righteous *ex eo* but not *coram eo*, they receive their righteousness from God but are not righteous when actually confronted with God: "Nihilominus etiam iusti sunt, sed ex eo, non coram eo. . . ."[13] This example may serve to show the radicalness of Luther's thesis that the sinner through the grace of Jesus Christ stands justified *coram deo* and confident in Christ (*fiducia*), that incorporated in him through Baptism, he can look joyously forward to the coming of the Lord in glory.

This vision of the *fides Christo formata* is not an isolated or secondary point. We may conclude this section by quoting from the 1536: "Disputation on Justification" where Luther points to the pivotal nature of the teaching that "it is necessary that we make satisfaction for actual sins. This is a popish doctrine, and those holding the very same view invented manifold ways to reconcile God. We see that this argument is the fountain and source of all monasteries, Masses, pilgrimages, invocation of the

[12] For documentation, see my *Harvest of Medieval Theology*, p. 311. For a further discussion, see my "Schrift und Gottesdienst: Die Jungfrau Maria in evangelischer Sicht," *Kerygma und Dogma*, X (1964), 229–45; synopsized in *Journal of Ecumenical Studies*, II (1965), 332.

[13] *Sermones de tempore*, edited by J. M. Mandernacht (Cologne, 1863), Sermo V, 9, p. 494.

Saints, and similar devices by which men try to make satisfaction for sins." Earlier in the disputation he discusses the need of good works, springing from faith, and he states clearly that "our obedience is necessary for salvation." Such a statement may explain why there is in our time an inclination to believe that the doctrine of grace and justification is no longer a dividing factor and that a consensus is about to be reached. Though perhaps ecumenically inspired, such a belief does not take into account the completely different context in which Luther—and with him the whole Reformation—places this "necessity of obedience." According to the Reformation view this obedience and the necessity of good works do not form the missing link in the lifeline between God and Christians; this is firmly and completely had in Jesus Christ. They function, rather, in the realm of man and fellow-man and are therefore not *heaven*-directed but *world*-directed and in this instrumental way glorify God and build his Kingdom.

IV.

This horizontalization of grace and the works of grace leads us to a few final comments on the relevance of the Reformation doctrine of grace for the "Secular City."

The relevance of a seriously taken doctrine of predestination for modern man, threatened with being lost in the anonymity of mass existence, we mention only in passing. Our discussion is limited here to the question whether the so-called pessimism of Protestant anthropology is not a decisive obstacle to communication with "a world come of age," conscious as it is of its communal and individual potentiality, as, for example, expressed in the dream of the "Great Society."

In an effort to characterize Augustinian theology Etienne Gilson indicated as one typical aspect that "when there are two equally viable solutions of one and the same problem, an Augustinian doctrine will spontaneously go for the one which assigns less to man and more to God." [14] With his Thomistic point of view

[14] *Introduction à l'étude de saint Augustin* (2e éd.; Paris, 1949), p. 317 (my own translation).

Gilson is hardly able to hide his disregard for such a position. A parallel criticism has been aired time and again with regard to Reformation theology. The Reformers have been taken to task for a seesaw theology which was incapable of elevating the glory of God without debasing the nature of man.

Two considerations might help to clarify this issue. In the first place Reformation theology is indeed Augustinian in this respect that it has basically opted for the backward stance of St. Augustine's theology, developed as it is from the point of view of the stage of justification and peace with God reached in Book X of his *Confessions*. Looking back upon his life he confesses that it was God's continuous grace which overcame his human rebellion and opposition in order to lead him to his conversion. The prevenience of grace—yes, the irresistibility of grace—anchored in God's efficacious call and predestination, is a confession of the sovereignty of God. Theological thinking is viewed here as *sacrificium laudis,* as doxology.

The mediaeval development of theology from the *sacrificium laudis* to the *sacrificium intellectus,* from doxology to docility, was determined by the change from the backward stance of a confession theology to the forward stance of metaphysical theology. This transition is marked by the shift from the confession of God's sovereignty to speculation about the relations of predestination and free will, or of grace and nature. We do not intend to suggest that St. Augustine himself would not have contributed to this shift in stance nor that it would not be important for the Church to place next to a *confession* theology a *pastoral* theology and *apologetic* theology which employs metaphysical categories to express its faith. At the same time it should be clear that predestination and free will, grace and nature seen as *alternatives* makes for a seesaw oscillation which is alien to confession theology.

A second consideration is relevant here because the question may arise whether St. Thomas and his representatives in the contemporary *nouvelle théologie* have been able to reconcile predestination and free will, grace and nature. It is indeed clear that in this Roman Catholic tradition there is no danger of false contrasts and alternatives and that here there is little evidence of a seesaw oscillation.

To understand the Reformation position, we have to turn to what may seem a technical, perhaps even a typically Scholastic problem. Nevertheless it proves to be a problem of far-reaching implications, especially as regards the relevance for the contemporary "Secular City." According to Reformation theology, the original righteousness (*iustitia originalis*) in which Adam was created was not a supernatural gift or a preternatural gift but was part of the nature of Adam. In one of the older dogmatics one can find the concise question and answer: "Cur dicitur [iustitia] originalis.—Quia naturalis fuit et primus homo in ea et ad eam conditus fuit. . . ." [15] *Iustitia originalis* can be translated as "completely pleasing to God." [16] Consequently, in the Fall the nature of Adam took the full brunt of the impact of sin. This doctrine has led to the reputed Protestant anthropological pessimism. According to traditional Roman Catholic teaching Adam was created with nature plus supernature—specially added gifts which constituted original justice. Consequently in the Fall Adam lost his supernatural gifts but was not completely corrupted, although wounded in his nature: *spoliatus a gratuitis, vulneratus in naturalibus*. This allows for a seemingly more optimistic view of man.

The attrition resulting from the confessional cold war in the last centuries has obscured the real issue to the extent that Protestant theologians increasingly emphasized the total corruption of man as if this were a doctrine in its own right (one of the so-called "fundamentals") and have encouraged Roman Catholics to believe that Protestant theology was caught in the *perpetuum mobile* of the seesaw.

In this last section we should like to point out that what seems somber pessimism from the point of view of hamartiology, actually opens wide vistas of promise and hope from the point of view of redemption and the coming kingdom. Man *himself* and his *very nature* carries the promise of redemption; the man who is redeemed

[15] "Why is this called original justice? — Because it is natural justice and the first man was thus and hereto created" (Wilhelm Bucanus, *Institutiones theologicae* [Geneva, 1609], X, 6; quoted by H. Heppe–E. Bizer, *Die Dogmatik der evangelisch-reformierten Kirche* [neuarb. Aufl.; Neukirchen, 1958], S. 192).

[16] "Vollkommene Gottwohlgefälligkeit" (Heppe–Bizer, *ibid.*, S. 175).

134

is the same as the one who is created. Grace does not elevate nature nor does it transcend nature. Rather, grace sets man free and re-establishes him as "completely pleasing to God." Often we have thought about redemption too anthropocentrically and not seen that in Adam the whole of creation was at stake. Through the Fall the whole universe became a "victim of frustration"; and ultimately "the universe itself is to be freed from the shackles of mortality and enter upon the liberty and splendour of the children of God." [17] The Christian expectation is "earthy": it looks forward, not to a supernatural existence, but to a "new heaven and a new earth."

Such a view of the relation of nature and grace, of creation and redemption does not allow for the construction of alternatives, contrasts, or a seesaw, but is able to express the sovereignty of God and the glory of him reflected in his creation, now hidden, but soon to be public and visible. From this point of view the divine mission of the State can be reasserted to replace the mediaeval contrast between the Church as supernatural society and the State as natural society.

Ultimately more important, however, it allows us to break down the dangerous wall of partition between the two Testaments. The supposed superiority of the New Testament on the grounds that it showed man's supernatural end, usually contrasted with the Old Testament message as limited to man's natural end, has done more than any other single factor to alienate Christianity from the "Secular City." The Reformation understanding of grace and redemption can thus contribute to our ecumenical growth and provide contemporary New Testament Christianity with a new access to the surrounding secular world as the creation of God. The recovery of the Old Testament is so essential that it may be said that the only avenue of approach to the modern "Secular City" runs via the fourth city, Jerusalem.

[17] Rom. 8:20, 21 (The New English Bible).

Index